John E. S. Otty.

THE CHURCH AND THE DIVINE ORDER

BY THE SAME AUTHOR

VISION AND AUTHORITY; OR, THE THRONE OF ST. PETER. Crown 8vo, cloth, 7s. 6d.

THE PROBLEM OF FAITH AND FREEDOM IN THE LAST TWO CENTURIES. Large crown 8vo, cloth, 10s. 6d.

LONDON: HODDER & STOUGHTON

THE CHURCH AND THE DIVINE ORDER

BY

JOHN OMAN

HON. M.A. (CANTAB), D.D. (EDIN.)

AUTHOR OF
"VISION AND AUTHORITY," "THE PROBLEM OF FAITH AND FREEDOM," ETC

HODDER AND STOUGHTON

LONDON NEW YORK TORONTO

BRITISH ISLES NAZARENE
LIBRARY
COLLEGE

PREFACE

THIS whole discussion will appear to many a pure anachronism. When we are in the throes of deciding whether our society is to rest on individual competition or legal socialism, what does it matter, they ask, whether men belong to one Church or many or none at all?

Regarded as spiritual facts, however, what is now called individual competition and legal socialism are not opposites at all, for both alike are simply organised force. Where in our present industrial system is the personal dealing of man with man in trust, friendliness, and consciousness of mutual benefit, which makes relations individual? The attraction of socialism for serious thinkers is precisely the greater hope of baptizing organised force in the State, than organised force in the limited liability company, with righteousness to all and consideration for the weak. Yet even the ideal State of the socialist would remain to the end organised force; and the long, weary struggle of history has no meaning, if force, however organised, can conserve man's highest interests. The only hope of socialism lies in teaching men that their economic position, and all the outward goods force could conserve, are subordinate interests. With that, a time might come when food and raiment were as much common property as water and air. But man will never consent to pool his supreme interest, and if that be possession, there would only be the old result even from ideal socialism. When "he that gathered much had nothing over, and he that gathered little had no lack," the people cried, "But our soul is dried away, there is nothing but this manna before our eyes."

Yet, if competition must continue, and society continue with it, it must become individual in another sense than at present. Organised individualism, heedless of brotherhood, mutual helpfulness, the duty of the strong to help the weak, and the grace and joy of life itself, is only a specially brutal anarchy. Hitherto it has only been tolerable at all because a great many influences from an order in which love is the fulfilling of the law, have descended upon it.

Only as we manage to subordinate organised force to this higher order of love and freedom will it be our servant and not our slave-driver; and merely to change its form will not serve us. That order a prophetic remnant alone may serve, but by them all forms of social order must be saved, whether individualistic or collective. In some order of love and freedom, that is in some kind of Church, the historical struggle of mankind must be gathered up, and, if it is not being served by the present Churches, then a supreme effort should be made to recall them to their true task. Only in a very dim sense are they not of the world, which seeks personal gain and is divided by rank and possession, but they all contain elements of self-sacrifice not to be found elsewhere; and except by self-sacrifice no social salvation will ever be won. That many are falling away from them is true, but that may be their gain, for, when they become religious societies, holding men only by religious ties, their true object and power will appear.

Having these convictions, I have felt the

history of men's thoughts regarding the Church worthy of renewed study. The strange thing is that none of it is really past, but that somewhere every phase of it is still active, no one of us, perhaps, having wholly escaped the influence of any part of it; and I have tried to tell the story in the proportion of its interest for the problems of our time, especially among those who speak the English tongue.

My obligation to books, so far as I was immediately conscious of it, will be manifest from what I have written, save two valuable papers on Augustine's Neoplatonism and his conversion by the Rev. W. Montgomery, which have not yet come into possession of the public. Perhaps I should also emphasise my obligation to Sohm and Loofs. Next to them, I am more indebted to many discussions with my colleague, Principal Skinner, than to any writer on the subject. Mr. Walter Hobhouse's "Church and the World" came into my hands too late to influence any of my conclusions, but it has impressed me as a sign of hope to find myself so much in agreement with a writer of another Church and another way of thinking on other subjects.

Finally, I desire to acknowledge the kindness of my friends, Mr. G. W. Alexander and the Rev. F. W. Armstrong, in reading the proofs.

JOHN OMAN.

WESTMINSTER COLLEGE, CAMBRIDGE.
1911.

CONTENTS

THE JEWISH PREPARATION

CHAPTER I

THE JEWISH PREPARATION

THIS new study of so old a question as the Church, a question which has already called forth much more learning and ability than the present writer can claim, has been prompted not merely by its practical importance at this time when Christians of various denominations seem prepared to consider anew their mutual relations, but by the belief that no good can be accomplished till we recognise that our differences do not concern the Church but the doctrines of God and of salvation upon which our views of the Church rest. Arguments about the Church can only end in barren logomachies so long as we are not at one about what manner of God we believe in and what manner of salvation from Him we expect.

In the preparation for the Church this

dependence upon the ideas of God and of salvation which it enshrines is already apparent. The Church, as the highest and widest fellowship among mankind, was prepared for in some degree by every form of human association, but the association in which we see its direct ancestry is distinguished by ideas of God and salvation, not by organisation. Indeed, failure as worldly organisation was often the source of its power as spiritual leaven, the failure of the national ambitions of Israel being the very thing which turned men's attention from a national to a religious hope.

From the time of the earlier prophets the failure to unite the tribes for any lengthened period began to awaken a sense that true unity lay deeper than outward union. Amos of Judea prophesied in Israel, and denounced woe both "to them that are at ease in Zion and to them that are secure in the mountain of Samaria"; Hosea found the goodness of both nations as the dew which goes early away; Isaiah of Jerusalem was influenced by no one more than Hosea the prophet of Israel. Thus religious fellowship surmounted external divisions. After the Exile had brought all political unity to an end, the conception of a unity depending on the immediate care of God found noble expression in the prophets, especially the second Isaiah. Later, a yet wider breach of outward unity took place. "The Dispersed of Israel" had no longer a common speech. Most of them spoke Greek; and if they knew Hebrew, it was as the dead tongue of the sacred writings, and not as the language of their people; while Jerusalem was for them a religious and no longer a political capital.

Among this scattered people arose the most important of all outward preparations for the Church—the worship of the synagogue.

The whole religious life of the synagogue seems to have grown up remote from the immediate influences of the legal scribes and the temple ritual. The teacher took the place of the priest, ritual had no part in the worship, and the national aspects of the law were more and more subordinated to the broadly human. In an important if small section, there was positive antagonism to the legal ceremonies and revolt against the sacrifices.

Even in the synagogues of Galilee these influences were at work, and it was everywhere from the synagogue and not from the temple that Christianity extended itself. To seek the nature of the Christian Church in any connection with the Jewish priesthood is to contradict all the historical evidence. Not with the institutions associated with the temple, but with the spiritual preparation associated with the synagogue was its fellowship.

The worship of the synagogue did not cut off the Jews from intercourse with the many peoples in the wide Græco-Roman world as the temple ritual would have done, but allowed them a freedom of intercourse which created a new sense that God had made of one blood all nations. Interest was thereby diminished in what was merely national in their religion and deepened in what was human and universal. Then, as they realised how it met the common spiritual need of mankind, they were taught to set a new value on their religion for what it taught of God and required from man. Consequently the Jewish religion was never more universal in its outlook or more missionary in its activities, never nearer passing from the stage of a national creed into a Church than at the moment when its heritage began to be transferred to the Christian community.*

The deep significance of the synagogue for the rise of the Church lay, therefore, not in its organisation, great as that influence may

* Bousset, in his "Judenthum," discusses later Judaism entirely from this point of view. It derives, he thinks, its significance from being a movement which went half way towards becoming a Church. The creation of a Church requires, he says, (1) That the religion begin at least to be separated from the national life of the people. (2) That not individualism but new forms of religious association arise. (3) That the religion in this form begin to pass the limits of the nation. He quotes Strabo in Josephus (xiv. 115) to show the extraordinary extension and influence of the race at this time, and Paul (Rom. ii. 17–21) as a masterly description of their temper. Their exclusiveness was not softened nor their demands lessened, yet, in the joy of propagating their religion, they opened wide the doors of the synagogue. Matt. xxiii. 15 shows their zeal to make proselytes even in Palestine. There the question of Gentile converts divided the schools of Hillel and Shammai, and the exclusiveness of the latter did not prevail till bitterness against the Roman power had grown strong on suffering, while amongst the Diaspora it did not arrive till after the destruction of Jerusalem. Not till then did the Jews become haters and hated of all, as Tacitus describes. Having failed to become a universal religion and being no more able to be a national religion, Judaism became a religion of observances and absolute stationariness, and Christianity absorbed the more liberal spirits and went on to do the work Judaism had failed to persevere in.

have been on the organisation of the Church, and not in its societies, large as the opportunities they may have afforded for the propagation of the Christian faith, but in its approach to a universal religion. In short, they embodied the prophetic task of Israel, in which supremely the preparation for the Church of Christ is to be sought.

As Loisy says, "Jesus gathered up and vivified the best of the religious wealth Israel had amassed before Him, and to deny that and isolate Him in history is not to make Him greater, but only less intelligible and less real." * Now this treasure was mainly prophetic. From the beginning the prophetic revelation dealt with one thing: a people, however few, who should say, "Not by might, nor by power, but by My Spirit, saith the Lord." They are the seven thousand who have not bowed the knee to Baal, by whom the prophet was taught that the Lord is not in the storm but in the still, small voice; the remnant who abide when violence has done its worst; the servant of the Lord who by silence and suffering is the redemption of Israel. They are a people who have learned the folly of potsherd striving

* "The Gospel and the Church," Eng. tr., p. 137.

with potsherd, and above all of a potsherd striving with its Maker.

The prophets had only learned that hard lesson by being driven in on their own souls and there learning what was universal and eternal. The fact that the burden of prophecy was for the nation, is apt to make us forget the still more important fact that this burden was laid on one man's soul. All the elements of Israel's religion were influenced by that sense of a soul directly dealing with God. The manifest national purpose of the law obscures the extent to which even in the Proverbs the rule of life has reached a common human standard, which, though often only of common sense and sometimes only of common shrewdness, is, nevertheless, individual and universal. Prophecy has its natural result in Ezekiel, with his teaching that every man shall die for his own sins and only his own. Still more manifestly Job stands on a purely human and universal basis. Last of all, the Psalms set forth a simple worship of the heart which continues to speak to the spiritual needs of mankind. Here we find the preparation which delivered men from the temporal and national to find in their own hearts and in their fellow-men the universal and the eternal, and so enabled them to receive the thought of association purely on the ground of belief in one God and one salvation for all His children.

But prophecy, we are reminded, ended in Jewish apocalyptic. And that is set forth to-day as both national and material. This idea of an actual Jewish kingdom to be introduced by the finger of God is being used as the master-key to unlock all doors in the history of the time, an exaggeration which is apt to withdraw our attention from the profound moral and religious connection between the apocalyptic hope and the Christian conception of the Church.

This connection is indicated in the very name of the Church, the *ecclesia.* It is the ideal Israel, the body of the elect, now oppressed and obscure, but to be manifested with Christ in the kingdom of God. Upon the apocalyptic hope of the early Church all the triumphant feelings associated with the word rested. The way in which the word is used in the New Testament in different connections, and apparently with different applications, only means that the real signification was ideal. The word was not first applied to the local communities and then extended to the whole, but stood, from the first, for the New Testament Israel. Its application to the local communities only asserts that the essence of the whole was in every part, that wheresoever two or three were gathered together there the Church was in all its power and in all the promise of the kingdom of God. Sohm, to whom the credit of emphasising this idea is due, has thus expressed it: "The faith of the Christians sees in every Christian assembly gathered in the Spirit the whole of Christianity, the people of God, the total community. On that ground every assembly of Christians, whether small or great, which met in the name of the Lord, was called *ecclesia*, an assembly of the New Testament Israel." *

For this depth of meaning the first cause must be sought in the belief in the resurrection. The Church was the fellowship of the glorified Christ. His headship meant that this fellowship, this New Testament Israel, was endowed with a power which need not consider outward might, whether of men or evil

* Rudolf Sohm, "Kirchenrecht," i. 18.

spirits. But that, again, was prepared for by the apocalyptic expectations.

Whatever earthly, or even national form it may have assumed, whatever Roman or other tyrannies it expected to see overthrown, and whatever kingdom of immediate divine control it expected to see granted to Israel, the religious essence of it was still the old prophetic idea of a holy remnant to whom earthly might is weakness and meek acceptance of God's will alone strength. Nor could its aims be primarily political when its method was so entirely religious and anti-political.

It rose no doubt from the Greek oppression, but the Maccabean revolt, even while it succeeded, becoming more worldly and fuller of political and social compromise, and in the end, in spite of all worldly devices, failing to work so much as political salvation, men's hopes turned more exclusively to a kingdom of heaven. "They dreamt of a fashioning of the earthly existence into the likeness of the world of the angels and the stars."* That expectation, no doubt, had a temporal form, an expectation of a near and

* Baldensperger, "Das Spätere Judenthum als Vorstufe des Christenthums" p. 20.

sudden introduction of the divine order. Yet what it spoke to was a religious temper which felt all temporal forms to be necessarily subordinate and all material forces necessarily temporal. "The flight into the supersensuous is with strong religious personalities inseparable from a retreat into one's own heart."* Thereby the Messianic hope began to be separated from a political idea of restoration, and to be connected with spiritual hopes which only God could realise, and which in the end left men alone with God and the divine, the prophetic, order of the world.

After all, non-political persons do not cherish merely political beliefs, and those who cherished apocalyptic hopes were the "quiet in the land," those who, by patience in suffering, had been taught the might of God's rule, and who, through grievous disappointment, had learned not to trust in man. Quotations may be found and so interpreted as to support the view that it all ended in crude material hopes, but no apocalyptic writing as a whole means any such thing. The soul of apocalyptic is the old prophetic belief that power is on the side of those who are on God's side, and that He is

* *Op. cit.*, p. 19.

not to be found in the thunder and the tempest, but in the still small voice. The prophetic assurance has become more definitely apocalyptic only in the sense that all expectation of this new order is entirely from the introduction of God's rule by God's hand, and not by human efforts and human institutions.

Now the Church is the society which believes in that rule of God and in no other. Apocalyptic in that sense is the nerve and sinew of Christ's teaching, and His significance for the Church is that He so entirely made the Father's rule man's sole environment, even to death and the cross, that it was possible for even the humblest believer to make faith in it the adequate basis of fellowship.

The Church, no doubt, had an expectation of an immediate *parousia*, and the restoration of all things, and under that immediate expectation it began its journey with an enthusiasm and a freedom from the perplexities and compromises which a long struggle in the world always brings, but it was able also to do without the temporal form, precisely because, through Jesus, faith in God's own rule was no more a matter of time's incidents but of an immediate sense of God which still sustained in them the belief that love and not power is the final order of the world, that indeed in the last issue love alone is the irresistible might, the one thing which knows us altogether, and which in the end we shall altogether know.

In this apocalyptic hope—it matters not in what temporal or material envelope it may have been encased—we do reach the final religious order. Religion has to do with what has been called the conservation of worths.* It will secure to all eternity the blessings upon which men believe their lives depend. But the first lesson of life is that much men value is by its very nature merely fleeting. Consequently the task of conserving becomes preeminently the task of discriminating what can be conserved. Progress in religion thus comes to be largely a matter of rejection. The lower religions seek to maintain life's most material goods. A spiritual religion only arises when it is discovered that the things of the body are all corruptible, and that only the things of the spirit can be eternal. An ethical religion begins when it is discovered that of the things of the spirit only what is righteous can be eternal. A universal religion begins

* H. Höffding, "Philosophy of Religion," p. 6.

by rejecting what is national in this righteousness, and retaining only what is human, individual, universal.

This rejection, however, turns out to be no mere negative process, but the discovery of the true meaning of life. Mankind in its journey has, through stress of conflict, had to reject one part of his baggage after another. This surrender, however, has been like the story of the Sibylline Books. The more there was destroyed the more valuable the rest became, for the more it showed the true meaning of the world and the more it enabled man to put to right use the temporal as well as the eternal. It is this practical loss and gain which distinguishes religion from a merely intellectual, philosophical search for the permanent amid the fleeting.

The last stage in this process must be the meekness which brings everything down to God's rule of love, and, by so doing, inherits the earth. Primarily that religious basis of the Church had no source but the original and undivided religious consciousness of Jesus, and it only continues to exist where faith is sustained and quickened by His spirit. Apocalyptic may only have been a negative preparation, bringing the religious problem down to the lowest point of making God's rule man's sole environment, but it was a negative preparation which summed up the whole prophetic task and no man can understand the positive message of Jesus without it.

A large part of the Church's failure throughout the ages has just lain in her failure to understand the prophetic and apocalyptic preparation. When authority and compulsion seemed a sure and quick road to truth and unity, it was difficult to regard the Church as other than a worldly corporation, and to remember that she stood for God's rule in however few, and by God's way of the patient endurance of love, however long. It is the things Christ does not trust in, which men have been so slow to learn.

"*ECCLESIA*"

From Deuteronomy onwards συναγωγή is used to translate *édā* and ἐκκλησία for *qāhāl*. In Jas. ii. 2, συναγωγή is used for the ordinary gathering of the Christians, whereas in Rev. ii. 9 and iii. 6, compared with ii. 8 and iii. 7, ἐκκλησία means exclusively the

Christian assembly and *συναγωγή* the Jewish. Yet the selection of the word *ecclesia* was not due merely to the fact that *synagoge* was already appropriated for the Jewish assemblies, for already a more ideal sense was connected with the former word. Before usage had determined the application of *ecclesia* to Christian assembly and *synagoge* to the Jewish, *synagoge* seems to have meant the local community, the visible congregation, and *ecclesia* the ideal Israel. Schürer says, "*συναγωγή* expresses only an empirical state of things, while *ἐκκλησία* contains at the same time a dogmatic judgment of worth" ("The Jewish People in the Time of Christ," II. ii. p. 59). Sohm finds even in classical usage some difference of tone in the use of *ἐκκλησία* compared, say, with *ἀγορά* or *σύνοδος*; while in later usage it represents the people as a whole, were it only in tumult ("Kirchenrecht," i. 16 ff.). Wellhausen finds yet another cause for the preference of *ἐκκλησία*. The original Aramaic word *k'nishta*, he says, was applied to the Jewish as well as the Christian communities. But in Greek *ἐκκλησία* was the more distinguished word, and it may be that the Jew of the Diaspora had already exalted it above *συναγωγή*, which had assumed a limited and local sense. The etymology which made *ἔκκλητοι* equal to *ἐκλεκτόι* may have influenced the Christians in adopting it for exclusive use ("Evangelium Matthæi," p. 84). A trace of a wider usage seems to appear in Gal. i. 22. "All the churches of the Christ" would seem to mean that the Jewish communities might also be churches. On the other hand, "All the churches of the Christ" in Rom. xvi. 16, which Hort interprets as the

Churches of Judea, probably only means the churches of Corinth, which Paul had persuaded to distinguish themselves no longer as of Paul or Apollos or Cephas. But the expression which most clearly indicates the association of the word is "the Church of God" (1 Cor. xv. 9 and Gal. i. 13), which, as Hort suggests ("Ecclesia," p. 13), is a reminiscence of Psa. lxxiv. 2, and, therefore, a conscious annexation of the Old Testament conception of the congregation which God had purchased of old. Hort ("Ecclesia," p. 116) gives a summary of all the various uses, local and other, in the New Testament, but Kattenbusch ("Das Apostolische Symbol," ii. 692) supports Sohm's view that in all its applications it has the one meaning, the New Testament Israel. "The word in Matt. xviii. 20, 'for where two or three,' &c., was valid everywhere and of the whole Messiah. The *χριστός* is the head of the *σῶμα*, and this *σῶμα* is the *ἐκκλησία*. The use of the plural *ἐκκλησίαι* is to be compared with the use of *πνεύματα* in 1 Cor. xiv. 32, the spirits of the prophets, though there was only one Spirit. Each local community is an *ἐκκλησία*—not as a mere *συναγωγή* but as a representation of the whole."

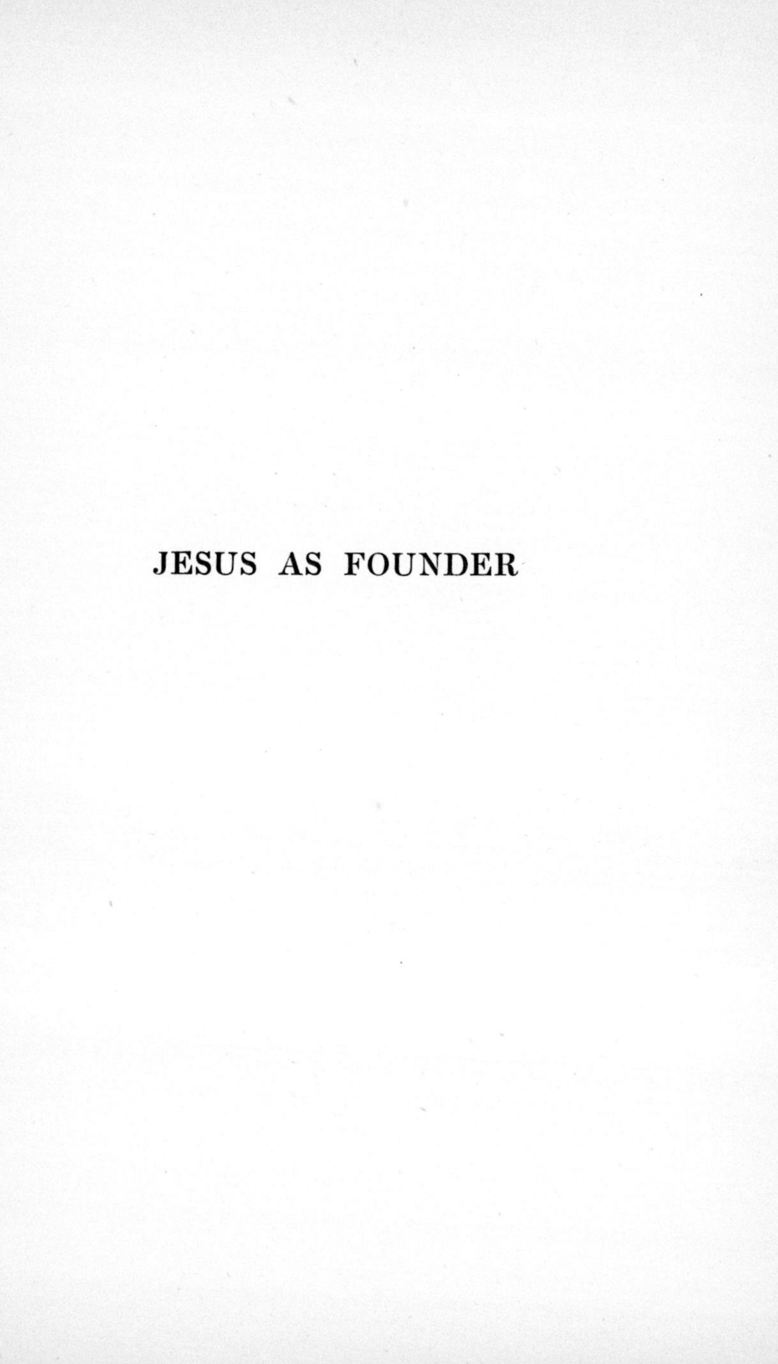

JESUS AS FOUNDER

CHAPTER II

JESUS AS FOUNDER

THAT Jesus was the inspiration which created the Church, and that the belief that He was in His exalted state its Head, caused it to continue, only extreme historical scepticism could deny. It is, however, very strongly denied that He ever founded it as an organisation, or even contemplated the continuance of His work in a permanent society. Above all, it is denied that He founded a society with officers having external authority and composed of members of mixed quality, such as the Christian Church actually became.

Three arguments are adduced. First, no authentic record of such a foundation exists in the Gospels. Second, His relation to His nation was such that He could not have meant to create a religious society apart from it. Third, His apocalyptic expectations allowed neither time nor use for such an institution.

These objections we shall consider in order.

First, no authentic record of such a foundation exists in the Gospels.

The discussion is concerned exclusively with the Gospel of Matthew. There we find that Jesus founds His Church on the rock either of Peter or of Peter's confession, that the gates of Hades shall not prevail against it (xvi. 18), that it is to hear accusations and rebuke wrong (xviii. 17), and that the disciples are to evangelise, baptize, and teach, and so gather mankind into an institution with observances and regular instruction (xxviii. 18–20). Then there are passages which seem to identify the kingdom of heaven with the mixed society of the Church. It is good seed among which an enemy has sown tares (xiii. 25), a net in which even the disciples' own labour will gather bad fish as well as good (*v.* 47), a wedding to which some come without a wedding garment (xxii. 3 ff.). Moreover, these passages have nothing to correspond with them in the other Gospels.

That one evangelist might be interested in a class of sayings which did not interest the others is seen from the absence of such striking parables as the Good Samaritan, the Pharisee and the Publican, and, above all, the Prodigal Son from all but the Gospel of the Gentile Luke. But Peter's confession is found both in Mark (viii. 27 ff.) and Luke (ix. 18 ff.), without any saying regarding the Church. If the passage in Matthew means that Jesus organised the disciples into a corporate society and appointed Peter head, the absence of it from Mark, which was written from Peter's preaching, or, indeed, from any narrative of the incident, would be fatal to its authenticity. It would then have been the outcome, the real significance of the confession, and omission would have been impossible. Hort argues that Church here does not mean a concrete, organised society, but the new Israel, the solid beginning of which our Lord finds in Peter's faith, not in His authority, for which foundation is no appropriate figure.* Such a reference to Peter, he thinks, is not of the kind which later ecclesiastical ideas would have created. Against this view it is urged that it involves a different meaning of the word in xviii. 17, where it must be a concrete assembly ere a case can be brought before it. There Hort would understand simply the local

* "Ecclesia," p. 9 ff.

meeting, Christian or, more probably, Jewish. As the words were used on different occasions, this difference of meaning is quite possible, and if it stood alone would be no ground for questioning the authenticity of either saying. But this understanding of the texts is just as much a rejection of the belief that Jesus founded a society with a mixod membership and superior officers as the rejection of them would be.*

The saying in xviii. 17, in any case, comes in strangely along with the command to forgive till seventy times seven, and the words about considering the obdurate man as a Gentile and a publican could only be in accord at all, if it

* Beyschlag, who takes the same view, thinks that the universal sense of xvi. 18 is harmonised with the local sense of xviii. 17 by the conception of the Church as the two or three gathered in Christ's name ("New Testament Theology," Eng. tr., i. 162). More recently the tendency has been to deny the authenticity of both passages. Holtzmann says that *church* does not mean anything which existed in our Lord's time, but in both passages the later Church, "the customs and rights of which the evangelist carries back to Jesus as the Deuteronomist the later constitution of Israel to Moses" ("Neutestam. Theologie," i. 212). Wellhausen argues that in both cases the evangelist means the mother-church at Jerusalem.

merely meant, think of him as outside the Church, a concrete state of things scarcely possible till a later date.

A comparison with the other Gospels creates the impression that the passages may contain genuine sayings, but with some adaptation to a later situation. The time of sleep when in Matthew (xiii. 25) the tares are sown, is in Mark (iv. 27) the time when the seed springs up. The good and bad in Matthew (xxii. 10) are in Luke (xiv. 21) the poor, halt, maimed and blind—moral wrecks but genuine converts, and (xiv. 16 ff.) those who are invited but are not of the spirit of the kingdom do not come in. The final commission is given in Luke (xxiv. 47 ff.) and also in John (xx. 22), but in far more general terms. Manifestly genuine teaching of Jesus has been modified unconsciously, and probably by use in exhortation, under the stress of a situation in which the Church was in theory still regarded as the society of the kingdom of God, and in actuality was rapidly becoming very unlike it.

That it should be Matthew, a member probably of the Jerusalem Church, who is exercised about the problem of mixed membership, is an important hint regarding the influence of that community on the course of future development.

The result is to show that "it is highly improbable that Jesus ever gave any positive precept directed towards outward separation from the Jewish community, or a formal, statutory constitution of a new community." *

All this does not, however, decide that Jesus never contemplated the existence of His followers as a separate society, and that He was never aware of the impulse which He gave them. This leads to the next position that has been maintained.

Second, That the relation of Jesus to His nation was such that He could not have meant to create a religious society apart from it.

Bousset thus states the position. "It was not His intention to found an organised community, a sect in opposition to the rest of the people. His mind remained directed to the great whole. With warm longing He laboured for His people to the end." † It is argued in particular that His last journey to Jerusalem, when He knew He exposed Himself to death,

* Titius, "Lehre von der Seligkeit," i. p. 172.

† "Jesu Predigt," p. 55.

can only be explained as a last appeal to the nation.

Had Jesus, as Bishop Gore maintains, all along had in view the foundation of the Church, and His whole training of His disciples been to make them the stable nucleus of this society,* a society which He marked off by appointing for it solemn ceremonies,† with a divine sanction attached to its legislative decisions,‡ with a hierarchy to keep it one, holy and catholic,§ there could never have been from the first any dubiety about separation from Judaism.

Instead of acting as men conscious of being the hierarchy of such an institution, the apostles continued to worship in the temple and observe Jewish rites. Only after grave searchings of heart, did they consent to receive Gentiles without circumcision—the mark of membership in the Jewish community. Even the insistence of Paul and the leadings of Providence scarce enabled them, to the close, to recognise the separateness of Christianity. Against such a founding of the Church the argument is undoubtedly valid that Jesus

* "The Church and the Ministry," p. 39.

† P. 40. ‡ P. 42. § P. 48.

regarded Himself as not sent but unto the lost sheep of the House of Israel (Matt. xv. 24).

But, while it is true that Jesus did not separate either Himself or His followers from Judaism, it is equally true that He deliberately created a different spirit which He knew would go its own road.

Ritschl traces through Mark a growing separation from Judaism. In i. 44 Jesus commands the leper to show himself to the priest and make the offering; in ii. 19–22 the disciples are not to fast, and that because the new revelation cannot be clothed in the old form; in ii. 23–28 the Sabbath is made for man, the disciples being free as members of the kingdom of God to judge all laws by the highest ends of man; in vii. 1–5 tradition is repudiated, and the whole conception of external cleanness on which the whole Mosaic ritual rested denied; in x. 2–9 elements in the Mosaic law are temporal and defective and not to be accepted by His disciples; in xii. 28–34 love to God and our neighbour is the substance of the law and all that need be retained for the kingdom of God. After that He could leave the full development of the Christian law and the withdrawing of His disciples from their ancestral worship to their future progress under the guidance of the Holy Spirit.*

If progressive purpose cannot be as easily traced in the other Gospels, the leading impulse from which our Lord's discontent sprang is at least as apparent. This was His feeling for man as man, for the toiler, the outcast and the alien, as children of the Heavenly Father. He begins to teach because He has compassion on the multitude as sheep not having a shepherd (Mark vi. 34). The morality of the Sermon on the Mount is given to the multitude, though it is a requirement above the righteousness of the Scribes and Pharisees (Matt. v. 20), and the burdened, to whom those high demands were to give rest, may have been those oppressed by ceremonial as well as by toil (Matt. xi. 28). The Spirit of the Lord God was upon Him, not for founding a new ecclesiastical institution of the type of Judaism, but for preaching the gospel to the poor (Matt. xi. 5), and His power to preach such a gospel crowned His claim to be He who should come, being higher than making the blind see or raising the dead.

* "Die Entstehung der Altkatholischen Kirche," 2nd ed., first section.

To the poor the highest religious life was now open, in comparison with which the official, orthodox person, the Pharisee in the temple, or the priest and Levite on the road to Jericho, was not religious at all. It is a life, moreover, which He never illustrates from religious observances, but always from the common life, and especially from the life of the toiler and the poor.

To those outcasts from the higher life of Judaism He adds the heathen. The only active reform of the national worship He ever undertook was the cleansing of the court of the Gentiles. Holtzmann traces a development of this sympathy, especially after He was driven from His own land and brought into personal contact with the heathen. How, Holtzmann asks, could it be otherwise with an ear so keen, a heart so sensitive to even the faintest voice of God in the world of men?* By such experiences as that with the woman of Syrophœnicia "the universal kernel of the thought of the kingdom of God burst its historically conditioned shell."†

The hesitation with which the mission to the

* "Lehrbuch d. neutest. Theologie," i. p. 231.

† P. 234.

heathen was entered upon by His disciples shows that this interest in the heathen was never wrought out by Jesus into a programme, but the irresistible spirit with which His religion triumphed over all racial prejudices and hindrances also shows how much mightier an impulse may be than a programme.

This impulse was primarily derived from a new doctrine of God, as the Heavenly Father, and of salvation, as acceptance of His rule in His power. The foundation was not a world-embracing institution, but a right relation to our Heavenly Father, and through that to our brethren. Yet it did involve a break with the old institution, because, first, its ceremonies were such as the poor and the alien never could perform, but such as condemned them to a lower religious level and to moral dependence; and, second, as the demands of it had no relation to the common human need of God and the common human duty of seeing God in our daily life and our fellow-men, they were as inadequate morally as they were burdensome ceremonially.

Indifference to washings and concern for a righteousness exceeding that of the Scribes, indifference to the traditions of men and concern for the purity of heart which sees God and the love which is the fulfilling of the law, Jesus must have known led far away from the Jewish national religion, and, for that matter, from all purely national ideals whatsoever. Nor does this merely prove the gulf between him and the Pharisaic party. It marks alienation from the whole legal organisation of Judaism. Not the Pharisees but the Sadducees, the official party, put Him to death, and mainly on the charge of having said, "I will destroy this temple that is made with hands, and in three days I will build another made without hands" (Mark xiv. 58). Whether actual words of Jesus or not, they describe exactly what He did, and He could hardly have been blinder than his foes to the consequences of His actions.

That he went to the temple and the synagogue, chose the religious festivals for His appeals to the people, and made his last journey to Jerusalem as a testimony to the nation is opposed to the view that His one task was to create the Church as a separate organised religious society, but is in no way inconsistent with the view that He placed His ultimate hope on His disciples and not on the nation.

All the Synoptic Gospels record the saying that new wine must be put in new bottles (Matt. ix. 17, Mark ii. 22, Luke v. 37 ff.). What might that mean if not that the new truth of His gospel would be certain to embody itself in new forms, and if these new forms were a rejection of the essential ritual of Judaism, He could hardly fail to see that it meant the creation of a new society. Yet it is equally manifest that He thought the new gospel would create its own organisation, and that His task was neither with its form nor its outward destiny, but solely with its spirit. Its form, like all other things of the morrow, He committed to His Heavenly Father.

The *third* objection, now regarded by a special school as the strongest of all, is that the apocalyptic expectations of Jesus allowed neither time nor use for such an institution as the Church.

In His lifetime, we are told, men expected not a Church, but the immediate appearing of the kingdom of God. The belief in the resurrection, and not Jesus, created the Church.* Jesus Himself is thought never to have

* Johannes Weiss, "Die Schriften des Neuen Testaments," i. 344.

overcome the particularism of the popular apocalyptic religion. The expectation of the rule of God meant for Him simply a renovated Israel. His belief in God as Father was circumscribed by that view, and he regarded Himself as the future Messiah, merely to introduce God's kingdom so understood. This kingdom He thought to be so near that He taught neither the people nor His disciples, as is generally supposed, but sent out messengers announcing, as John the Baptist had done, its immediate coming. The view that the apocalyptic of later Judaism spiritualised the national expectation, and that Jesus spiritualised it still farther into a faith which drew no hard distinction between present and future, thereby attaining gladness in life and an inward protest against a purely world-denying piety, is said to be a mere misinterpretation of an irony which by contemplating the shortness of the time, has forced its way through to equanimity.*

In answer it must be said first of all that no one ever gains any victory by a mere negation. No one has ever reached a forgiving spirit and freedom from worldliness

* Albert Schweitzer, "Von Reimarus zu Wrede." Eng. tr., "The Quest of the Historical Jesus," p. 247.

by the mere thought that the time is so short that he does not need to care.* When the keenest advocate of this position seeks to explain on this ground that all things shall be added to those who seek first the kingdom of God, he has first to ignore the context, which is not apocalypse, but consider the lilies, sufficient unto the day, ye cannot serve two masters; and then to vanish in a cloud of words.†

Second, the principle that Jesus must be interpreted from without inwards is not true, and it is the less true that in practice the application of this principle is taken to mean that the most material interpretation of His sayings and actions must *ipso facto* be most historical. To the creative mind has always belonged the great intuition, and the materialising of it has always come from the imitators and commentators. If the apocalyptic and the spiritual ideas are contradictory, it cannot be the apocalyptic which is most reliable. That Jesus had a sure spiritual penetration, given to none besides and incapable of being invented for Him, is a truth which

* As A. Loisy, "The Gospel and the Church," p. 81.

† Schweitzer, *op. cit.*, p. 247.

authenticates itself; while the ascription of crude apocalyptic ideas to Him by followers who certainly held them, is easy to explain.

Nevertheless, there is a vital and fundamental truth of Christianity underlying the eschatological view. Spiritual victories which men can still repeat could be no mere phenomena of "the exaltation of eschatological expectation." Yet there is a sense in which, to use Schweitzer's clumsy formula, "the affirmative can only issue from the superimposed negation." The victory over the world is by being prepared to lose it, the blessed use of life in being poor in spirit, the possession of our soul in the judgment of ourselves as sinners and in self-surrender. Jesus did not rest His kingdom on a basis of property and a civilisation measured by multiplied wants. This, as Brunetière says, is only possible for a few thousand citizens who live on the leisure which some millions of slaves have wrought for them, and the inspiration of it is not Christianity but Classical Antiquity.* The basis of the Church is precisely this denial of the world, this assertion that the meaning even of the world is not in itself or even in anything man can accomplish in the midst of

* "Essais sur la Literature Contemporaine," p. 72.

it, but in a blessing above and beyond only to be wrought out in the last issue by the finger of God. This temper is ascribed to the oppression and poverty which surrounded Jesus, and Protestantism in general, being absorbed in problems of wealth, politics and science, is apt to assume that, whether it exists in Christianity or not, it is not true. But, if we should rediscover our souls and with that, humanity, an enormous wealth resting on over thirty per cent. of abjectly poor, would seem more of a denial of God than Judea under the foreign yoke, for there poverty was never as inconsistent with the highest good of humanity. Then religion will once more need some kind of apocalyptic outlook, some sense that life is not good in itself, but only good when we overcome it through faith in a rule which God Himself will introduce.

Jesus founded the Church to live under that conception, as the society, in short, of the kingdom of God.

But it is argued that Jesus regarded the kingdom as so near that nothing was needed to fill up the interval. All His ministry is supposed to have been spent in a tense state of expectation that God would immediately bring the present world order to an end amid tremendous upheaval and judgment of the wicked. Matthew is supposed to be right in placing the saying, "Ye shall not have gone through the cities of Israel until the Son of man be come" (Matt. x. 23), early in His ministry. When the kingdom failed to come, He went up deliberately to Jerusalem to suffer, to bring it in. There He held a sacred meal with His disciples, not as an observance to be continued after Him, but as a seal of their reunion upon earth in the kingdom His sufferings were to introduce.

The belief in the resurrection is supposed to have altered all this. But, *first*, how did something so very different from the triumphant entrance of God's rule ever suggest itself, or how did it not end as all similar heated imaginings have ended, in harsh disillusionment? Further, in Mark xiii. 1–10, in a discourse which has every mark of genuineness, Jesus deprecates the expectation of a near end held by His disciples, warns them against false prophets, pictures them as a sufficiently visible company to be persecuted, declares the Gospel must first be preached to all nations, and only promises salvation to those who endure to the end. Then, His temptations have no relation to the mere proclamation of a catastrophe, but apply to the dangers of a lengthened moral and spiritual ministry. Nor is it right to exclude from Mark or to doubt that it offers the most reasonable expectation of His actions, that after His quarrel with the Jerusalem scribes, He did not again expose His life till He had retired for a time to teach His disciples (vii. 24 ff.). Still more convincing is the whole temper of His teaching, with its parables and interest in individuals and its whole air of leisure and detachment of mind. Last, and most convincing of all, is the conception of this kingdom, the laws of which are meekness and hungering after righteousness, purity of heart, and a child-like spirit. How could such a kingdom be introduced suddenly, by mere fiat? In view of all this, especially when we remember that He Himself said He knew not the hour, and that it was ever his habit to do what immediately lay to His hand to do and to regard the present as part of the future, we cannot suppose He was hindered from founding a society by the mere closing in of His time horizon.

The *second* difficulty is still more important.

The introduction of the kingdom is said to have been conceived by Jesus as so entirely a work of God that there could be no place for any society either to introduce it or to prepare for it.

Jesus did not, with the Catholic theologians, identify the kingdom of God with the Church, nor with modern theologians since Schleiermacher, with the progressive amelioration of humanity. It was something so present in Himself that the sons of the bridechamber could not but rejoice (Matt. ix. 15, Mark ii. 19, Luke v. 34), and the whole New Testament is a witness to the amazing strength and joyfulness which sprang from contact with His spirit. Yet this is not the final possession. The kingdom of God is, as Loisy expresses it, the realisation of perfect happiness in perfect justice and of immortality in holiness.* The Gospel is more than the restoration of the individual soul to the love of the Heavenly Father, being further the assurance that this love will one day have its perfect manifestation. Many passages, scarcely to be interpreted as metaphor, indicate that this belief had a setting in accord with the expectations

* "The Gospel and the Church," p. 122.

of the time, but the proportion of things is wholly inverted when that is put first, and the fatherhood of God and the conception of salvation are made to depend on it. "This is My beloved Son" was a religious experience before it was an endowment for pardoning sin and introducing the kingdom of God, and all the teaching of Jesus presupposes that a new relation to God must precede a new hope in Him. Willingness to subject the life in the present to the law of love is the imperative condition of faith in a future rule in which love shall have its perfect manifestation.

The kingdom of God, then, was something which needed to be prepared for, and yet could not be accomplished by any preparation. In the end it must be a regeneration of all things by the finger of God. But so far is that conception from making the idea of a Church impossible, that it is the very thing which made a new society necessary and which determined its type. It is to be a society which must ever judge itself as the brotherhood of the kingdom of God, not taking any thought for the amount of visible power it may have on earth, but organising itself wholly on the basis of love and leaving the issue to God. The fundamental conviction was that the true divine order is ever ready to break into the world, if men will only suffer it to break into their hearts. It was the society of those who already realised the blessings of the kingdom of God in their hearts—pardon, grace, joy—and were so sure that it would come in fullness, that they could live as if it were actually come. To see this is to understand why Jesus could leave so many things alone, and send His society into the world with no instructions except to be free from the fear of opposition and to avoid the kind of authority all worldly organisations think necessary to success.

In comparison with an ecclesiastical programme, this may seem the dream of a visionary, and only by possessing the spirit of Jesus can men ever think otherwise. But, without taking account of the inspiration of that dream, we shall merely find the history of the Church one of the least edifying accounts of worldly institutions.

The conclusion of the matter would seem to be that Jesus had no need to concern Himself about founding a society, but only to make sure that it was a society of the right kind. The society came into existence of itself, and very soon developed that feeling of a corporation which forbade a man to cast out devils "because he followed not us." That saying is not in Matthew, but in Mark (ix. 38); and it is to this society and its dangers, both from without and within, that we find many references in our Lord's teaching. The world would hate them, because they were to stand for something in the highest degree uncommon and unpopular, yet they would be everywhere hospitably received, because there would be souls prepared by God where they least looked for them. This society is not to be exclusive, as if no good could exist outside it (Mark ix. 39); it has to esteem the kindness which offers a cup of cold water, to guard the little one in the faith and the true life; it is not to fear sacrifices; and above all it must avoid personal claims. Every member, moreover, is to have salt in himself as well as to be at peace with others (Mark ix. 39–50). The possession of personal power is the sole and adequate organising force of the society. Service shall be the only title to authority, but authority shall involve yet humbler service (Mark ix. 35).

By precept and example this rejection of the type of authority by which all other societies are ruled is made prominent in all the Gospels. The fullest account is in Matt. xxiii. 8–12. Every clause authenticates itself by its vividness and point. Be not called Rabbi, for One is your teacher and all ye are brethren; be not masters, One being your master or leader; be exalted only through humility. Here is a society having the equality and mutual helpfulness of souls all alike taught of God.

With this conception the only official and the only ritual appointments Jesus ever made are in agreement. These were the selection of the apostles and the institution of the Lord's Supper.

The apostles, so far from being conceived as a hierarchy in germ, are called disciples, primarily because Jesus appointed them to be with Him (Mark iii. 14; Luke xxii. 28). They are only called apostles in connection with being sent forth on a special mission of preaching and healing. Mark carefully restricts it to one occasion—iii. 14, Jesus appointed twelve with a view to sending them forth (ἀποστέλλῃ); and vi. 30, apostles (ἀπόστολοι) on their return. In Matt. x. 2 it means "envoys," but also in connection with this mission. The word is found in John only in the indirect form "one sent" (xiii. 16). Luke (vi. 13, xvii. 5, xxii. 14) manifestly reflects a later usage. If there was any official title it was "The Twelve," and the only hint which suggests any connection even of it with the authority of office is the saying that they would sit on twelve thrones judging the twelve tribes of Israel (Matt. xix. 28, Luke xxii. 30). Whether the sense of that passage is symbolical or apocalyptic or a mixture of both would be hard to say, but the practical outcome of it is clear. The expectation is not used to justify a present claim to authority, but to require the renunciation of it. In Matthew it is followed by a parable which instructs the apostles to be prepared to give a place equal to themselves to later comers; in Luke xxii. 26–27 it occurs in connection with being unlike those who exercise political power and with the new order in which the greater is to be as the younger, the leader as the server, in accordance with the Master's own example of being among them as one who served and not as one who sat at meat.

With the Last Supper Luke connects the strife regarding who should be greatest. From Mark and Matthew we gather that this is a mistake. Yet in that case there must have been a reason for linking the incident to that solemn occasion. This impression is confirmed by the fact that John deliberately substitutes for the appointment of the Supper the washing of the disciples' feet. Manifestly he regarded that incident as setting forth the vital significance of the ordinance.

As this sacrament has more than aught else determined the character of the development of the Church, a right understanding of what took place in the Upper Room is important. What could not have been understood by the associations of the night on which Jesus was betrayed could not originally have been in the institution. As He was still present in His earthly body, one would imagine that there could be no conceivable room for speculations about partaking of His heavenly body. Nothing seems clearer than that the breaking of the bread refers to the breaking of His corporeal body and the outpouring of the cup to the shedding of His real blood, the symbolism being in the breaking and pouring, not in the material. It is only necessary to recall how constantly the Master's speech was in parable, to be sure that the disciples would never have interpreted the words literally. It was a parable even to the double form, the repetition with some deepening of meaning in the second member, to which they had been so long accustomed. To two things it refers —His own sufferings and the kingdom of God. On first announcing His sufferings, He set forth their significance. They are to enable men to lose their lives for His sake and the gospel's. These words, and not His teaching generally, are what men are tempted to be ashamed of in this adulterous and sinful generation (Mark viii. 34–38). Yet this sacrifice is victory, for the kingdom of God is also a feast shedding on this feast held under the shadow of the cross, joy and peace, so that weakness is turned into power. Thus the observance embodies all the contrasts of the Sermon on the Mount, in which the poor in spirit inherit the kingdom of God. Hence it is precisely what a feast should symbolise, a companying with the host and the obliteration of all distinctions in the sense of an equal and joyous fellowship. It was a rite which did not turn the officers of the Church into sacrificing priests, but sealed all His followers into a fellowship wherein the cross, in contrast with human power and authority, is the one mighty thing through all eternity. Thus the view of it which continued down to Augustine, as the Church offering up herself through Christ her head, is not far from the original meaning. That spirit and not ecclesiastical rites or forms Christ impressed upon His Church with the solemnest words and the solemnest deeds, and this rite is simply the most solemn.

Instead of an ecclesiastical programme and an incipient hierarchy, we have, therefore, a society organised on the sole basis of love and equality and mutual service. This has been described as a dream which would have passed away like dew had not a Church with ordinary worldly rule early taken its place. The Church, it is said, also needed the preservative element of all society, meaning by that an authority in which the first is first and the last last. The Church organised like other societies is as necessary to the gospel as the gospel is to the Church.* In the Early

* A. Loisy, "The Gospel and the Church," p. 150.

Church the hierarchy is solely of devotion, but apparently it is pure advance when in a century or so it becomes the hierarchy of office.* One can only recall that the Master was once tempted to worship Satan, which is reasonably taken to mean worldly methods, in order to obtain the kingdoms of this world.

The point is also missed when it is argued that Jesus must have appointed for His Church authorities and an organisation, because He must have wished it to be a corporation and not a horde.† In His view the followers who receive His Spirit and believe His teaching cannot fail to be the most perfect community organised on the only divine, the only permanent basis, the rule of God which is love. That may seem a very unreal dream, but, as Loisy says, Christ's dream was His project.‡ And the question is whether, with the same sense of what God is and what salvation has to do with, it might not be still the only really practical scheme in the world. Perhaps nothing is

* P. 148.

† T. Strong, "A Manual of Theology," p. 323.

‡ Loisy, *op. cit.*, p. 122.

wanting to it except faith in the Father and His rule.

The society Christ founded was to be made one solely by being one with the Father through faith in Himself, whereby the power of the world to come should be so present in this life that all events in it should be found of His wise love and all the demands of it the assured way of victory and peace. A society with the power of the world to come thus working in it, naturally could not be served by any bond of visible authority.

THE APOSTOLIC CHURCH

CHAPTER III

THE APOSTOLIC CHURCH

WITH the apostles the Church went out into the world to struggle amid the clash of human interests and the compromises of human societies. The long Jewish preparation had not provided a nation, but only a few individuals capable of carrying on the impulse of the gospel. No one, it may be not even Paul, may have so perfectly responded to the preparation and at the same time so perfectly transcended it, as to be able to carry on the gospel in all its fullness. Yet the impress of Jesus upon the whole Apostolic Church was so immediate that it must be of primary importance to know (1) how the Apostolic Church conceived itself, and (2) what in actual reality it was.

First, its conception of itself. This was governed wholly by the belief that the risen

Christ was its Head. In that sense the belief in the resurrection continued, if it did not create, the Church. But the question is, what was the significance of that belief in the Headship of Christ? and that involves the further question, whether any change of view can be traced in the New Testament writings?

The whole amazingly joyous and victorious spirit of the New Testament witnesses to the strength of the conviction that the risen Christ was the Head of the Church. But it was not merely that He was thereby conceived as actively present for its aid. The resurrection was also the approval of God upon what He had been and the assurance that the order of humility and love He had founded was the eternal and victorious order. Peter assures his hearers that Jesus, being by the right hand of God exalted and having received the promise of the Spirit from the Father, had poured forth what was then seen and heard (Acts ii. 33). It was He who added to the Church (ii. 47). By Him signs were wrought (iv. 10). He appeared to Paul on the road to Damascus (ix. 5) and in the temple (xxii. 17). It is His Spirit which guides His servants (xvi. 7), is their strength in trouble (2 Cor. xii. 8), makes men saints in spite of much imperfection (1 Cor. i. 2), and bestows all the gifts by which the Church is built up (Eph. iv. 11). But the value of the resurrection is to Peter that Jesus as He had lived and taught and suffered is shown to be a man approved of God (Acts ii. 22), while to Paul it declares Him to be the Son of God with power, according to the Spirit of holiness. As men who had through Jesus seen the Father and realised their unity in a personal but common hope of His rule, they were, by the resurrection, assured that God is the last word in all events and that faith in Him is victory over the world and over sin. The crucifixion transformed into the resurrection taught that the last word of power is not human might but the Father's rule, so that we may be one with the Father even amid the hardest trials and the sternest duties.

The hope was probably made more than ever apocalyptic. The restoration of all things drew nigh. But it was a spiritual, not a material hope, and neither its spiritual nature nor the patience of God behind it were overlooked. Men must first repent and turn to God, and there may still be needed times of refreshing from the presence of the Lord (Acts iii. 19). Moreover, this hope was not at any time all in the future. Like all real spiritual hope, it rested on a faith which brought immediate succour. It is not only that the exalted Christ bestows present inspiration and help (Luke xxi. 15, Acts ii. 33), but we have all through the New Testament a sense that the eternal realities are faith and hope and love, and that in them we have an individual present possession which in the end could be summed up as having eternal life (John vi. 47, 1 John v. 13). Men believed that the power of the world to come was even now operative in the present world order, and in the last resort their faith was sustained, as all true faith must be sustained, precisely by finding help of God to live above and not by the present world order.

Most clearly we can trace the relation of the conception of God and of salvation to his conception of the Church in Paul. Through stress of controversy his doctrine of justification may have had a Rabbinical element in the form of it, but upon an understanding of the essence of it every renovation of the Church has depended. Its triumphant sense of God's purpose in our life and its glorious emancipation from fear of the law and all other fears which was the outcome of his faith in God through Jesus Christ, determined his whole view of the Church.

All who have been brought into this relationship of trust and freedom with the God and Father of our Lord Jesus Christ are saints. They may not be persons morally perfect or even morally advanced, but they are spiritual, related to God and open to the influence of His Spirit. Paul's doctrine, and with it the whole Apostolic doctrine of the Church, is that the Church consists of saints so understood. The Church is not a visible corporation, kept together by outward bonds of office and ecclesiastical order. It is a unity of spirit through the one Spirit of God working in the individual members, who, having been individually reconciled to God, are the spiritual who can judge all things yet themselves be subject to no human judgment (1 Cor. ii. 15). Because in this way Paul can say that Christ is the head of every man (1 Cor. xi. 3), he can say that we who are many are one body in Christ and severally members one of another (Rom. xii. 5). In 1 Peter ii. 5 the Church is for the same reason spoken of as a spiritual house, because it is composed through the Lord of living stones, of a holy priesthood, and still stronger in ii. 9–11 of a royal priesthood. The Church, then, is a society of those who are individually directed by the Spirit and need no other assurance of truth or bond of unity.

In Ephesians, however, it is maintained we have Paul's metaphor, but not Paul's meaning. In i. 22–23 Christ is said to be head and the Church His body, not, as with Paul, in the sense that Christ is the inspiring spirit of each member, but in the sense of being Himself part of the body. In v. 26 not the individual, as in the Pauline conception of justification, but the Church, is said to be the object of the work of reconciliation. Moreover, the conception of this headship is neither related to the kingdom of God nor interpreted through faith, but is mystical as the husband and wife becoming one flesh (v. 29–32), the consummation being conceived not as a work by the finger of God, but as the conclusion of a process (iv. 13).*

This interpretation has sometimes been ac-

* H. J. Holtzmann, "Neutest. Theol.," ii. 254 ff.

cepted without causing doubt regarding the authenticity of the epistle. Paul is supposed to have developed this more corporate idea of the Church as he meditated in prison at Rome, the centre of the world. But such a change would be an abandonment of the vital things in his early faith. The process which he found so powerless when it wrought through the Jewish society, he is not likely to have turned to in his old age merely because it wrought through the Christian society, and an experience which he had apart from the Church and by which alone he became a member of the Church is not likely to have been put last and the Church first.

The only question is whether a figure of speech is not unduly pressed. What is expressed collectively may derive its significance from what is experienced individually. The members are those who have been chosen in Christ before the foundation of the world to be holy and without blemish before Him in love (i. 4), and who are to have a spirit of wisdom and revelation in the individual knowledge of Christ (i. 18). Through individual holiness they are builded together for a habitation of God in the Spirit (ii. 22). By each apprehending the love of Christ they are filled with the fullness of God (iii. 19). By lowliness and meekness the unity of the Spirit is to be kept in the bonds of peace, and there can be one body because there is one Spirit and each is called into one hope, and the common possession is an individual possession of one Lord, one faith, one baptism, one God and Father who is the uniting force not only because He is over all, but because He is in all, meaning each. By individual gifts of grace the work of serving the Church is to be carried on, nor is unity to be the starting-point, or to be kept by any kind of submission or tutelage, but to be the goal by each attaining to a full-grown manhood (iv. 1–16). All this is manifestly in the spirit of Paul, and here we are not concerned to maintain anything more.

In the Pastoral Epistles, on the other hand, the Church is pillar and stay of the truth.* Faith is not a renewing trust in God through Jesus Christ, but acceptance of right Church doctrine † (1 Tim. i. 10). Paul himself derives

* Hort insists on translating *a*, not *the*, but it is certainly not *a* in the sense that there may be several others.

† τῇ ὑγιαινούσῃ διδασκαλίᾳ.

his authority from having the knowledge of the truth which appears to be sound doctrine (Titus i. 1–4). The Christian ethic is based on how men ought to behave themselves in the house of God (1 Tim. iii. 15). The heretic is a vessel of dishonour, and the whole conception of honour and dishonour is far away from Paul's conception of a body in which the uncomely parts have more abundant comeliness. Finally, in 2 Tim. ii. 21, Jesus is no longer Lord, but absolute master.*

It is difficult to escape the impression that we are here in the atmosphere of a later generation, an impression made deeper by the still ideal and individual conception of the Church in the Johannine writings. The only link with it is in Hebrews, where Jesus is described as a high-priest over the house of God (x. 21) and a crisis, caused by delayed hope, is bringing about a failure to realise the privileges of the Christian faith, though that faith is still, as with Paul, such a personal surrender to God as can be the personal proving of things not seen.

The *second* question is more difficult to answer. How was this conception of the Church realised

* Not κύριος, but δεσπότης.

in practice? What was the Church in actual reality? How far did this recognition of Jesus as Head ensure the continuance of His Spirit and the application of His teaching? What was understood by the two or three gathered in His name, by Jesus being the sole teacher, by all being brethren, by the first being last, and how did that teaching reflect itself in the actual Christian fellowship?

What Jesus left behind Him was a society in which no one counted that anything he possessed was his own, and which occupied itself with prayer, fellowship in the breaking of bread, and evangelising.

Socialism in the compulsory, political sense has no kinship with the teaching of Jesus, and in the stress of life this early community of goods was speedily modified. Yet the Church at Jerusalem was the first fresh, uncontaminated attempt to realise the spirit of One who had a common purse with His disciples, to whom privilege was no cause for pride of place, but for humility in service, who found the religious sphere in the common life amid common men, and who made love to God and man the sole law of His kingdom. That this spirit remained active in the Church is seen from the total absence of ritual precept in any of the apostolic writings and the unfailing fervour with which they all urge forbearance, brotherly kindness, and love.

From this spirit the idea of the unity of the Church as one universal body drew its power, and from that also it followed that the bond was not sought in any form of subjection of one person to another or of one community to another.

The apostles in some way must, of course, have been from the beginning the leaders of the Church. Jesus must have chosen them very badly, if they were not prepared at critical moments to accept responsibility and face danger. But, on the other hand, He must have impressed His teaching on them very inadequately, if they used the position that prominence would earn them to be a dominant caste within the brotherhood. What we read is that, having had special opportunities, they were in a special sense witnesses to the life and resurrection of the Master, that even for that end they left it to the community to choose, and to the Divine decision of the lot to select finally one to fill up their ranks, that they wished to give themselves exclusively to the ministry of the word, and that the only suggestion they make regarding organisation was the proposal to surrender the power of the purse, by handing it over to seven men specially elected by the community. Discipline in the ordinary sense they can never have exercised, for converts were not examined, but at once baptized, and the solitary inspired word of Peter to Ananias does not indicate any organised power of removing the unworthy (Acts v. 3 ff.). Soon we find them no college in any sense, but scattered abroad, content to be witnesses and missionaries to the whole Palestinian Church, in what Peter calls this ministration and mission (Acts i. 25). Naturally their influence must have been great at the beginning, and they could not avoid responsibility for the movements which arose. Yet these movements arose, and for the most part went their own way, without any scheme or policy of the apostles. Nor is it enough to say they had, and could have had, no successors. They were themselves speedily absorbed in the life of the Church, so that no corporate apostolic influence can anywhere be traced, but only the individual, personal influence of two or three.

Paul speaks of the persons he had to deal with as pillars, and he does not hint at the relation of any of them to the Twelve, or, indeed, speak of the Twelve at all except in relation to their chief task of being witnesses to the resurrection. Moreover, even these pillars are not persons whose actions are at all guaranteed for him by office, but they were, like others, persons whom God would not accept if they were wrong (Gal. ii. 6). No one had any office which, in his eyes, gave him any right over "the liberty which we have in Christ Jesus" (Gal. ii. 4). The result of the conference at Jerusalem was an arrangement which deposed the Twelve, individually as well as collectively, for ever from any central position they may have occupied in the Church, by withdrawing from their influence the whole Gentile community.

The supreme work of the Apostles was to maintain the spirit of humility which was the real bond of the Church. This was the task in which Peter was truly chief. He no longer girded himself and walked whither he would, but had to stretch forth his hands and allow others to gird him (John xxi. 18). He had been prepared by his Lord's own teaching to consider the Samaritans, but a Gentile proselyte he could receive as a brother only by Divine compulsion. Yet one who could be so compelled that he did not stop short of eating with that brother, had the root of the matter in him. Without attempting to justify himself either by office or by inspiration, he sought to carry the Church with him, purely on the ground of following the mind of God (Acts xi. 18). His inconsistency at Antioch, though deserving all Paul said of it in the way of rebuke, was governed by two right Christian impulses—the desire to recognise every brother in Christ as in all senses his brother, and the fear of alienating from the cause his brethren according to the flesh. It would appear from 1 Cor. iii. 22 that he took Paul's rebuke with Christian humility, and it was that spirit and not any authority of office which surmounted every barrier of race, language, caste, and religious prejudice, and made all believers feel themselves one in Christ Jesus.

The difference in Paul's bearing is usually ascribed to a different theory of Christianity. But quite as much was due to the very human reason that Peter lived far enough away from the Gentile and so near the Jew that his heart failed him when he came to face the ultimate issue of the common brotherhood of men in Christ in which both believed. To Paul also it was no small matter to put any obstacle in the way of the Jew. He is willing to be anathema from Christ for his kinsmen according to the flesh, but he is not willing to sacrifice the amazing experience which had broken down, in his own heart first of all, the distinction between circumcision and uncircumcision. It is part of his faith to know that his task is to cherish the actual practical fellowship of all believers, and to leave the consequences with God. At no time did he ever start from the idea of unity and from it attempt to attain brotherhood, yet he was never indifferent to unity as the goal of brotherhood. Though he never dreamt of being overruled by the desire for mere outward unity, and never thought of seeking it by surrendering his convictions, he made every effort to carry the Jerusalem Church with him. Concern for the practical needs of its members became for him a dominating interest. His last journey to Jerusalem in face of danger was a further effort after mutual understanding. His purifying himself in the temple with four men who had a vow, on the advice of James and the elders, is sometimes regarded as an invention of the author of Acts to prove more submission on Paul's part than existed.

Taking his epistles in the order Gal., 1 and 2 Cor., Rom., we see how the development of events seem to him to justify less need for assertion and more for conciliation; and if it were an inconsistency, Paul as well as Peter was capable of an inconsistency of the heart. The final serene victory is seen in Philippians. He has abandoned nothing of his conviction. "We are the circumcision who worship by the Spirit of God, and glory in Christ Jesus, and have no confidence in the flesh" (iii. 3). To see this is a mark of perfection. Nevertheless, the issue is not to be forced, but to be left to God to reveal. Meantime, the supreme concern for each one is to be true to his own convictions (iii. 15, 16). That spirit, and not unity of organisation, was the true bond of the Apostolic Church.

Harmony within and influence without were thus based on the profoundest individualism ever attempted in the world. This was made possible by a gospel which was at once the most personal of all possessions and the mightiest force to break down worldly and even religious selfishness. That which marked off the Church from the world was a gospel bringing to the individual pardon and grace, inward peace, spiritual power, and future hope, but it was also the gospel which made the Church such a united missionary force. Paul's generous words on the Jew who is one inwardly (Rom. ii. 29) and the Gentiles who show the works of the law written in their hearts (ii. 15) prove that he held no such exclusive view as *nulla salus extra ecclesiam*, but there was a glad sense of possessing in a special degree a salvation which made it a joy to bring men into the fellowship of the Christian society. In short, the Church was still, with the Messiah, the suffering servant of the Lord, the holy seed in the midst of the earth. In it the prophetic idea had at length been incarnated.

So soon, however, as men were brought in, they also had found their souls and came into such a relation to God and their fellow-Christians and were so saved into God's own rule that they had the liberty of the children of God and could be under no tutelage. The apostles themselves wrote and spoke from no pedestal of authority, but simply as those who most fully and gratefully recognised the blessings of membership in this society, as themselves humble members speaking to their fellow-members. Paul's attitude was, so far as we can trace, the attitude of all the apostles, "Not that we have lordship over your faith, but are helpers of your joy; for by faith, *i.e.*, by your individual faith, ye stand" (2 Cor. i. 24). He expects submission for the common good, but only such as he himself renders (2 Thess. iii. 7–9).

The same spirit rules in the relation of one community to another. Not through any recognised leader, but by the gospel manifesting itself through the ordinary members, the community at Antioch came into existence. The relation of this community to the parent community at Jerusalem we can best trace. The Church at Jerusalem, and not merely the apostles, being interested, sent Barnabas. There is no hint that he was sent to do anything but what he did do, rejoice when he saw that the work was of God, exhort the converts to fidelity, and further the work by helping and seeking others to help. There is no hint that he considered himself in any sense a plenipotentiary.

At a later date this community at Antioch felt themselves free to enter on larger enterprises without consulting any other body of Christians. The commission to send forth Barnabas and Saul came apparently to the whole community. They are described as engaged in serving the Lord, probably in prayer,* as if the work had been already laid on their hearts, and they were solemnly laying the matter before the Lord (Acts xiii. 1 ff). Naturally the Church at Antioch sought to carry with it afterwards the sympathy of the Church at Jerusalem in an enterprise that meant so much for the whole Church, but Paul makes it quite plain that it was in no sense an appeal. The answer came from the apostles and elders with the whole Church (Acts xv. 22). It is offered as what had seemed good to the Holy Ghost and the whole community in which He dwelt—a manifest reason why it should also seem good to the Church at Antioch which was equally guided by the

* λειτουργούντων τῷ κυρίῳ.

Spirit. The whole congregation at Antioch gathered to hear, and they received what had been sent, not as an ecclesiastical rule, but as encouragement (xv. 30–31). Moreover, the mere fact that Paul continued to seek an understanding with the Church at Jerusalem shows that he did not regard it as claiming the right of a metropolitan Church to direct the policy of its inferior. If more evidence is needed we have only to remember how Paul everywhere appointed elders in every Church and then left each new community to work out its own life, and the constant references in his epistles to Churches as brotherhoods commended to other brotherhoods simply by every tie of Christian love.

This question of the local community and its relation to the Church as a whole is bound up with the question of what was meant by office in the Early Church.

The boundaries of the local community must in most cases have been indefinite. Where two or three were gathered in Christ's name, there was the Church. In most cases it could be nothing but the meeting of the two or three in private houses. Even in Jerusalem the elders seem to have met in the house of

James (Acts xxi. 18), which probably means they had no public meeting-place. On Paul's initiative, the Christians at Ephesus withdrew from the synagogue and formed an assembly of their own in the school of Tyrannus (Acts xix. 9), but even there the Church can scarcely have continued to be one definite congregation meeting in one place. In Corinth there were various assemblies which Paul speaks of as "all the churches of the Christ" (Rom. xvi. 16), and which were of sufficiently different types to wish to call themselves by different names (1 Cor. i. 12). But the most certain proof of this freedom of assembly and indefiniteness of organisation is that we find Ignatius in the beginning of the second century still combating it.*

Nevertheless, all the assemblies were uniform in seeking to walk after the transmitted type (2 Thess. iii. 6),† *i.e.*, not according to a body of doctrine, but according to the right type of Christian conduct. They also followed common customs and observances (1 Cor. xi. 16 and xiv. 23). No community is to proceed as if Christianity had begun with it or ended

* "Ad Magn.," iv.; "Ad Eph.," xx., &c.

† κατὰ τὴν παράδοσιν.

with it (1 Cor. xiv. 36). Finally, the ministry of the word, baptism, and the eucharist exist in all Churches, being ascribed directly to the appointment of the Lord.

But all this unity was of the spirit and not of official regulation. The ministry of the word itself depended, not on an appointment, but on a gift. The classical passage on this subject is Eph. iv. Each possesses some measure of the gift of Christ; but for the building up of the body of Christ special men have in a special degree the gifts to be apostles, prophets, evangelists, pastors, and teachers. Upon the two former in particular the Church is built (ii. 20), because God now makes known His will through the holy apostles and prophets in the Spirit. By their task of leading men into the unity of truth, and not by the task of officials compacting them into unity of organisation, the body builds itself up in love. In Rom. xii. 6–9 Paul gives a still wider scope to the *charismata*, so that it includes also giving, ruling, and showing mercy. Yet prophecy is still first, the interpretation of God's mind being the fundamental idea of it. As the apostle is the highest possessor of this gift, it is manifestly not regarded as purely or mainly ecstatic, but is the gift, however exercised, of making men directly sure of the mind of Christ. Hence a Church built on the apostles and prophets is built directly on God's word communicated by His Spirit. Even in the "Didaché" the apostle is specially the prophet. His power is being limited, as he must not stay more than two days, but while he stays he apparently displaces the bishop in presiding at the communion (xi.), and, as one who speaks the Word of God, he is to be honoured as the Lord, for "where the teaching of the Lord is given, there is the Lord" (iv.), exactly as in Ephesians.

The prophet's gift in the Early Church was exercised mainly at the assembly for worship, though there each man had the right of speech, and some women took it. From the synagogue which had long been the nurse of the religious life of the Jew, weekly worship, public prayer, public instruction, and mutual edification passed with the converts into the Church, even to the liturgical form in some of the prayers and the saying of Amen by the hearers.

Most visibly the Church was distinguished

from the synagogue by the sacraments of baptism and the Lord's Supper, and though the administration of them was later the chief title to office, there is in the New Testament no trace of restriction to any class.

But if the ecclesiastical boundaries were vague, the circle of Christian influence was very definite, and baptism was the overt act of breaking with the heathen society and entering a society which was a new spiritual world. An ecstatic descent of the Spirit seems for a time to have been regarded as the normal beginning of the Christian life (Acts ii. 1 ff, viii. 16, x. 44, xix. 6), and as confession and baptism were simultaneous, this phenomenon frequently accompanied baptism. Yet Paul's indifference to its administration, compared with his insistence upon faith, shows that faith, not baptism, was, for him at least, the real channel of grace. As the essential thing in the Lord's Supper was fellowship with each other in Christ, Christians being the one bread, the one body (1 Cor. x. 17), and to partake in love being to discern Christ's body (xi. 29), we have two rites which mark off the Church as a fellowship of saints, of persons possessing God's Spirit, and so brought into unity with their brethren.

What the office of elder or bishop exactly was will occupy us more fully in the next chapter, but meantime it is important to realise what it was not. It cannot have constituted a body with any kind of legal authority. Nothing could be more impressive than the absence of any appeal to authority—the elders, the apostles, his own—in the crisis about which Paul writes in 1 Cor., when not only the unity but the purity of the Church was involved. What he ordains in the Churches is only an appeal to weigh well what others have found good (iv. 16–17), the rod with which he may have to come to them is not ecclesiastical discipline but the opposite of love and a spirit of meekness (iv. 21). The long discussion ends with the noblest appeal in all literature, the appeal in chap. xiii. to the spirit of love, which was not written as an appeal in the abstract, but as an appeal for the only true unity. There is no hint of any solution by submission either to teacher or official. The sole appeal is to a fuller corporate because individual subjection to the rule of love. Whatever office may have been in the Apostolic Church, it was capable of being subordinated to that ideal.

But a far more important matter than the organisation of the apostolic Church is the conception of God and of salvation on which it rested. That is summed up in the apostolic benediction, "The grace of our Lord Jesus Christ, and the love of God, and the fellowship of the Holy Spirit, be with you all." When the threefold name appeared may be uncertain. The formula in Matthew is rendered doubtful by the absence of it from the final commission in John, by Paul speaking of baptizing only in the name of Christ, and by the ease with which the later practice of the Church could be read back. But there is no good reason for questioning the blessing itself at the end of 2 Cor., because it is prepared for in 1 Cor. xii. 4, where Paul speaks of diversities of gifts but the same Spirit, diversities of ministrations but the same Lord, diversities of workings but the same God who worketh all things in all, and because it is no theological formula but the expression of a religious experience, the essence of which is what he speaks of in Rom. viii., as God sending forth the Spirit of His Son in our hearts crying, "Abba, Father," and the knowledge that all things work together for good to them that love God. In Christ the two things which are apt to go far apart—our experience of life and the aspirations of our heart—are brought into one. We are able not only to have the hope of a life beyond, but to have the security of it in a present life wherein reconciliation to God has meant reconciliation both to our trials and to our tasks. Christ had meant that practically, and His grace meant that a man found his true self through God's love in his life, and the fellowship of His Spirit in his heart. It was not an influx of God, obliterating the boundaries of personality, but a revelation of God which could make even the publican and the harlot heirs of God and joint heirs with Christ. The splendour, the sacredness, the inviolability of the moral personality was not only Christ's discovery, but His creation. Upon that basis the order of freedom, love, and service which Christ had founded still stood secure, and our frequent failure since to maintain it is due less to the difficulty of the task than to the deficiency of our faith in the revelation upon which alone it can rest.

THE RISE OF THE CATHOLIC CHURCH

CHAPTER IV

THE RISE OF THE CATHOLIC CHURCH

FEW historical questions are more important or more difficult than how the simple fellowship of the apostles in the first century was transformed into the Catholic Church of the Roman Empire in the fourth, with its hierarchy, its authoritative creed, its fixed traditions, its sacramental powers. The central problem is the development of the bishop.

If elders and bishops were ever the same, it is important to learn how they came to be distinguished; and, if there were at one time several bishops in one church, how there came to be only one. But more important than the exact development of the office of the bishop is the conception of office which was attached to it. How did any office come to be regarded as essential to the very nature of the Church as a Divine institution, as a part of the scheme of salvation? When that question is answered, the rest is simple, because as soon as opposition to the bishop was regarded not simply as a possible breach of the requirements of love and humility, but as directly and in itself a sin, the rest followed naturally. When the foundation of the Church was no longer the apostle and prophet, no longer the teacher with Divine gifts speaking to people with the gift to recognise them, but a fixed tradition expressed in an official appointment, the Church was no longer one in a prophetic hope of the future, but one by an organisation based upon the past, and that was the essence of the change.

The primary question, therefore, is how the official became prominent as the prophetic office declined, for in that change the whole idea of the order of the Church was necessarily involved. The prophet had been the special interpreter of the mind of God. What he said, therefore, had the irresistible weight of being the Divine Word. It was, like conscience, imperative, but like conscience also, it had no might except right, and the prophet could win no obedience except by persuading the Church that he interpreted aright the Divine mind. Consequently, he never could have any appeal except for love's sake. Moreover, he interpreted God's mind anew for each occasion, and in view of future tasks, not of claims of the past. It was, therefore, essentially an office to be judged by the service of the kingdom of God as its demands came upon each man day by day.

But the bishop was not God's interpreter merely. He was God's appointment, having by virtue of office the right to obedience. He could command, not merely persuade, and that in view of a past, an established order, and not merely of the future, the Divine order of God's own rule. The way towards unity in faith and fellowship no longer passed under the low portal of love and humility, but returned to the old high-road of visible legal authority. The first no longer needed to be last as in Christ's order, and the idea that all the potentiality of God's rule was present where two or three were gathered in the name of Christ lost its meaning.

All explanations agree in thinking the bishop increased because he was permanent and the prophet decreased because he was occasional. The answer is obvious and adequate, provided they were both concerned with the same task.

Most writers, however, maintain that from the first they were appointed for different purposes. The prophet was a teacher, the elder or bishop an administrator. The advance of the bishop must, then, be sought in such matters as his control over the Church's gifts or over admission and excommunication. But we are not thereby helped to understand how the official took the place of the prophet as one who spoke for God, and how the very belief in the Spirit of God, which before meant that all should judge, now means that all should obey. It is the old order, but so transformed, so travestied, that God's administrator asks unquestioned submission to God's appointment and does not depend any more on those who, being spiritual, discern God's Spirit. His sanction is legal and no longer purely religious, and how that could take place under the gospel of Jesus Christ is the problem.

Hereafter, whether to agree with him or not, every serious student of the subject must take account of Sohm's explanation.*

In his view bishop and elder were never names for the same office. The eldership as an office in the Church began in the second

* "Kirchenrecht," p. 92 ff.

century. In the New Testament and the Apostolic Fathers the elders mean simply the more experienced male members. Bishops are sometimes called elders, but that was only because they were naturally selected from these honoured persons, and elders "appointed as bishops" is understood where bishops are called elders.*

* Most writers follow Ritschl in holding προιστάμενοι, πρεσβύτεροι, ἐπίσκοποι, ποιμένες, ἡγούμενοι names for the same office. From Acts xx. 17 and 28 Sohm argues that Paul calls together the elders who were appointed bishops. Unfortunately for the argument all the elders appear to have been called and all turn out to have been appointed overseers. How when Paul appoints elders in every Church "as bishop" is understood, or how the senior members in Jerusalem could all gather in the house of James, he forgets to explain. When he argues from 1 Tim. v. 17–20 that the elders who rule well could not have been bishops, because elders who rule ill would, on the view then current, have ceased to be bishops, he overlooks the fact that it is precisely to decide whether they have ruled well or ill that there is to be an inquiry; and surely it is not because they are old, but because they are officials, that so much circumspection is required. But his chief reliance is on 1 Clement. In i. 3 he takes elders, young men and women to be an exhaustive classification of the community. No one questions that elders might mean elderly people. The question is whether it had also a special sense. And in that special sense, moreover, it is used here, for Clement is not classifying, but is contrasting young and inexperienced persons of both sexes,

None of the passages he cites can be read in that way. The bishops are early found surrounded by elders, and the theory that these elders began to be elected in the second century is without a shadow of proof. Hence it can hardly be questioned that the same persons were called elders from the qualities of wisdom and experience required for the office, and bishops from its task of oversight. Sohm, moreover, accepts a plurality of bishops in each Church, and even thinks they were of so indefinite a number that one could be added at his own desire. After that the name is of little consequence, for we have still the same problem to explain—how the one bishop came to be distinguished from the many—and whether the many were called elders or bishops matters little.

A more important question is raised when

whose proper sphere of rule is at home, with the rulers who are to be honoured because they hold the office of presbyters. In xliv. 4 and 5 there could be no sense in saying that the departed elders are blessed because they cannot now be expelled from the episcopate, except the work of oversight were identical with being an elder. Finally, in liv. 2, where he reads elders "who were appointed bishops," the natural reading is "because appointed."

he argues that the bishops never formed anything like a managing committee, and that the Church never was a body ruled by elected representatives acting together. For this view he relies on three arguments. (1) This would have been an ecclesiastical, legal order of the nature of political rule, whereas the very rationale of the Christian society was that it had nothing to do with *Recht*—that is, legal rule. (2) The Church was a charismatic society—that is, a society founded on individual possession of the Spirit—and a committee cannot have a *charisma.* (3) If the government of the Church had been in that sense democratic it never could have become aristocratic.

If the meaning of this view is that the Church could have no body of leaders taking common action, we have only to recall that the Twelve suggested to the Church the election of the Seven, that the Seven were a committee of distribution, a thing hardly possible without consultation and common action, that a committee of apostles and elders discussed the admission of Gentiles and at least made suggestions, and that Paul addressed the elders of Ephesus as persons having corporate responsibility. Moreover, the congregation described as "the multitude"* acted in a corporate capacity which, the moment it went beyond a very modest size, could only have been through representatives. Seeing facts have to be taken in history, not as they ought to be but as they are, that answer might suffice. But the difficulties themselves may also be met. (1) The legal quality of a rule depends on the spirit, not the number, of those who exercise it. (2) A board may not be able to have a *charisma*, but it might be made up of those who have, and there is a special presence of the Spirit in the assembly of the two or three which is not in the one. (3) Democratic in the sense that right could be a question of numbers and not of the mind of God, the Early Church never was, but where each member was a king and priest unto God it must have been democratic in the sense of the value of each member for determining what God's mind really was. History leaves no doubt that the significance of the individual is only felt strongly at heroic moments, that this can pass and democracies become autocracies,

* το πλῆθος (Acts vi. 2, 5; xv. 30).

sometimes with amazing rapidity. Wherefore, nothing has been yet said to disprove the prevailing theory that when the sense of the priesthood of all believers grew dim the representative character of their leaders gradually became of less account, their president came to have more power and became permanent, and so the monarchical bishop had his first beginnings.

But Sohm is on surer grounds when he proceeds to argue that the *charisma* for ruling never was distinguished, in the way Ritschl, Hatch, and others suppose, from the *charisma* for teaching.

The bishop, he maintains, was in the strict sense of the word no more elected than the prophet, but the special gift of both alike had to be recognised by the community before it could be exercised. The Holy Ghost had appointed the elders at Ephesus bishops. The recognition of this appointment, Sohm considers, was through the prophet, the usual channel of the Spirit's utterance. Then it was confirmed by the recognition of the community. Thus the gift, the *charisma*, which Timothy is to stir up, was pointed out by the prophet as well as confirmed by the laying on of the hands of the elders (1 Tim. iv. 14).

This prophetic election, moreover, was to a prophetic office. The charismatic, prophetic teaching gift was not always available, but experience, purity of life, and Christian love were, and they also were a special *charisma* for serving the Church (Rom. xii. 3). As the teaching gift required also the gift of love, the gift of love carried with it the right to testify. Hence we find the bishops occupied with the whole cure of souls, and they are early described as pastors (Eph. iv. 11, Acts xx. 28). This relation to the prophetic task makes it far easier to understand how the bishop came to claim by authority and in right of office to speak for God, as the prophet had done by inspiration and the appeal to the Spirit of God in every believer.

The most important element in this development, Sohm holds, was the right to preside at the eucharist. It was originally an offering, but of prayer and gifts, which was only later transformed into the bloodless repetition of the bloody offering on Calvary. The bishop or his representative was regarded as alone in a position to present this offering as well pleasing to God. By that position as receiving the gifts for Christ and presenting them to Christ, and not, as Hatch has supposed, by virtue of being finance minister of the congregation, the bishop came to take the place of the prophet and to be the representative of God. Nothing else, Sohm maintains, contributed so much to the idea that the whole potency of Christianity, which in the apostles' time was found in the two or three gathered in Christ's name, was now embodied in the bishop alone, as this task of presiding at the eucharist, offering the eucharistic prayer, and receiving in place of Christ the eucharistic gifts.*

Seeing Paul appointed no other means except the elders for carrying on the activity and worship he created, this account of the relation of the elder to the ministry of the Word must be much nearer the truth than that the prophetic teacher belonged entirely to one side of the Church's life while the elder as an administrator belonged exclusively to the

* P. 206 ff. He adduces chiefly 1 Clement, such passages as xliv. 3 and 4, but this idea of the sacrament continued down to Augustine and the place the gifts had threatened to take appears from the argument in the "De Civ." xxi. 27, against those who think that sins accompanied by almsgiving will do them no harm.

other. This identity of service would go far towards explaining how the value once assigned to the special gift for speaking through the Spirit in the name of God could be transferred to the bishop in right of office, seeing that his also had been a prophetic gift which had made him a representative of God from the beginning. By its relation to the eucharist this gift was changed from being prophetic to being official, and the rest followed.

Furthermore, the idea of unity may have had its special organ in the elders or bishops from the beginning. No account of their origin is given. As they do not appear to have been a development of the Seven, it is improbable that they were called into existence to manage the gifts of the Church, at that time its only material possession. Nor is it probable that they were appointed primarily to preside at the eucharist. The bread was broken from house to house, where the natural president would be the family head, and from the irregularity of the proceedings as depicted in the tenth and eleventh chapters of 1 Cor., there would appear to have been observances with no president at all, long after the eldership was certainly in existence. As individual teachers and leaders they may have arisen quite simply and naturally to take the place of the apostles who were scattered abroad by the persecution. But the question is, how do we find them at an early date the leaders of the Church in a way the Twelve had never been? They are already a body of representatives,* yet they are not representa-

* In Sohm's view the local community in Primitive Christianity was so entirely regarded as a mere aspect of the whole ecclesia that it could have no independent expression or act through any body of representatives. The practical issue would be that Christianity could have no common order and no corporate activity at all. Harnack ("Entstehung u. Entwickelung der Kirchenverfassung u. des Kirchenrechts," 1910, p. 166) rightly objects that this judgment of itself by the local community as embodying the whole ecclesia did not exclude but determine complete self-dependence. Moreover, Sohm himself, especially when he comes to explain the rise of the Roman power, has to assume at times the reality of the people's choice and the representative character of the elders. Yet Harnack's criticism (pp. 121–86) misses the true element in Sohm's contention. Ecclesiastical authority, in the strict sense, is the reversal of Christ's order. Sohm's error is not in denying the right of such authority in the Church, but in confusing all common action through representatives with that order of ruler and subject. Not the kind of representation, whether by many or few, and still less representation in itself makes a legal order, but

tives in a way which would indicate an origin either from the synagogue or the civic assemblies which, as Sohm says, would in either case have meant representatives chosen to administer with legal power. That kind of official would not have been in accord either with the spirit or with the indefiniteness of organisation in the Early Church.

But that spirit of brotherhood and the vagueness of the external bond might themselves give the elders representative character. The Church at Jerusalem was once small enough to meet in an upper room. When increase of numbers and persecution made a common meeting-place impossible, would the spirit of unity in the Church have permitted their fellowship to be broken up without any attempt at intercourse? And what other fellowship than by representatives could have been possible in the circumstances? Under the pressure of that need the representative character of the elders might spring up spontaneously. We can imagine an indefinite body consisting at first of persons like James

the spirit in which it acts, the spirit of wishing to be first in power without being last in humility and service, and of appealing to other motives than love's sake.

in whose houses the scattered worshippers met, which only as the desire for fellowship led to common action would become definitely representative. Thus there would be no account of the first appointment, for the simple reason that there was no definite first appointment to relate. The chief proof of this view is that in the New Testament the elders always represent the Christianity of whole cities, in most of which, as in Corinth, there were many churches. Such representation of local fellowship would in a practical way have been representative of the one Ecclesia. The bishop would thereby be associated from the beginning with the idea of unity, which makes it easier to understand how fellowship with him came to be regarded as the one sufficient mark of belonging to the one Catholic Church.

The actual disappearance of the prophet before the bishop can be traced, especially in the "Didaché." The first fruits are to be given to the prophets, if they exist, for "they are your high-priests" (xiii.). The prophet may order a table (xi. 4)—apparently a relic of the time when the bishop retired before him and he presided at the eucharist—but he may not eat of it himself. And his interference is to be a very temporary affair, because, if he tarry more than two days, he is a false prophet. Most illuminating of all is the injunction that the congregation elect bishops and deacons (both plural) to perform for them the service of prophets and teachers.

In the first epistle of Clement there are still several bishops in the church at Corinth, and by inference at Rome (liv. 2). Some of these bishops the Corinthians have removed. Against that proceeding this letter came from Rome as a remonstrance. The inference is that the bishops had already obtained at Rome the position which this letter claims for them at Corinth. To revolt against the bishops is sin (i. 1), even blasphemy against the name of the Lord (xlvii. 6–7). To remove them, if they have fulfilled their office blamelessly, is no small sin (xliv. 3, 4). The apostles appointed bishops, so that the appointment of all bishops is a divine ordinance, and what the bishops do is from Christ, and Christ is from God (xlii. 1–4). The charismatic nature of the office is so far remembered that it is said the apostles only appointed those they had tried by the Spirit (xlii. 4), but manifestly the authority is rested on office and no more on prophetic gift, while at the same time the prophetic claim to speak for God now clothes the bishop.

In the epistles of Ignatius we find for the first time only one bishop. Only he, or one appointed by him, may administer the eucharist ("Smyrn.," viii. 1). Only where he is with the elders and deacons is there a right assembly ("Magn.," vii. 1, "Trall.," vii. 2). Where the bishop is, there is the catholic Church, there—meaning there alone—let the multitude be ("Smyrn.," viii. 2). The catholic Church does not yet mean the Church as a whole, but the Church in its wholeness, the Church which has all the power of Christianity because Christ is there. But it is now the presence of the bishop as His representative, and not the fellowship in faith of the two or three, which guarantees His presence. That change of view contains in germ the whole change from Apostolic to Catholic Christianity.

The insistence and heat of Ignatius prove that this order was still new and was still opposed. Had not some continued to maintain that the catholic Church was where two or three were gathered together, he would not have been driven to the patent sophistry, "If the prayer of one with a second have such power, how much rather that of the second with all the Church" (Eph. v. 2). His whole purpose is to suppress such gatherings. No unity is acknowledged except unity with the bishop. All outside of it are schismatics, wanting the altar and deprived of the bread of God (Eph. v. 2). On many occasions they are exhorted to return, as if these simple gatherings of Christians were the innovation—a way not unfamiliar with ecclesiastics.

The bishop is not yet a successor of the apostles. He is a type of the Father ("Trall.," iii. 1). Among the presbyters, he is as Christ among the apostles ("Trall.," iii. 1, 2). Moreover, he has this position only in the local community, not beyond. Manifestly, therefore, he derived it not from succeeding the apostles in office, but from taking the place of one who had a *charisma* to speak for God.

Where this rise of the single bishop took place is not definitely known. As Ignatius mentions several bishops of churches in Asia Minor, but none of Rome, most writers have inferred that the single bishop originated in Asia Minor. But Sohm's view that this silence shows that the office had already a security in Rome, which it still lacked in Asia Minor,* is far more probable, as Ignatius could hardly have spoken of Rome with such unqualified panegyric, had it lacked the order upon which he is never weary of insisting. It may well be, therefore, that the single bishop originated in Rome itself. Indeed, it is difficult to see how from any other centre it could have spread so easily and so rapidly.

In what manner this change came to pass is equally uncertain. But after this idea of the significance of the bishops had begun to take root, their number would naturally be brought as low as possible. Anything which might make one individual prominent among the other bishops would bring nearer the time when one was first and distinct from the others. But if bishops were those who, presiding at the eucharist, represented Jesus Christ, they would become an august body to whose number additions would only be made in the very last straits. Also we can understand how election to the eldership would go on, but no one would be elevated from the ranks of

* "Kirchenrecht," p. 168.

recent appointments to preside at the eucharist so long as one of those revered as representatives of Christ remained.

The position of presiding at the eucharist may, therefore, have afforded occasion for the development of the authority of the bishop. Yet Sohm's conclusion "that from a hierurgical priesthood a hierarchical was born," is no truer than the opposite that from a hierarchical priesthood a hierurgical was born. Very early the heathen conception of holiness as something mysterious and wonderful may have been attached to the sacrament, and the president may have derived some mystical, even magical respect from being associated with it. But he was still only one who on behalf of Christ received sacrifices, not one who offered them. Even his position at the sacrament was more hierarchical than hierurgical, and not till long after his position had been assured as the source of order, unity, and truth, was he regarded as a sacrificing priest.

By the end of the second century the conception of the Church as a hierarchical society had begun, and by the middle of the third century it was complete. But the sacramental power of the bishop was only then beginning to be asserted.*

Yet from the time when the Church was founded on the bishop, not the prophet, from the time when it became a corporation with ruler and subject, the eucharist could no longer be the festival of the amazing fellowship where all were equally brethren of Christ, all equally kings and priests unto God, all set by Christ's obedience unto death free from the fetters of time and chance, and all enabled for the service of His kingdom to be partakers of His sufferings, that they might also be one with Him as heirs of God, and where all a man was and all he had could be an offering of thanksgiving.

* Irenæus, though regarded as the first Catholic theologian, the first who in face of Gnosticism appealed to the one Church as the ground of truth, and who considered that the bishop had a *charisma veritatis*, still held the old view of the sacrament (IV. xvii. 5). But already in his time the presbyters, as representatives of the bishop in presiding at the eucharist, are described as *συμμύσται*, and Clement of Alexandria ("Alex. Strom," vi. 13) opposes to the idea of a presbyter being righteous from ordination the idea of being ordained because he is righteous. Apparently Cyprian affirms this gift of a special righteousness when he says "cum episcopo presbyteri sacerdotali honore conjuncti," but the view was not held by Augustine, and he does not even contest it as if it were the generally accepted view.

Then the offerings which at one time had been the spontaneous expression of this sense of equal brotherhood in Christ's sufferings and triumph, tended to be looked on as in themselves a sacrifice and to become the essence of the eucharist. The God who received the gifts through the bishop and the salvation which He gave as an external gift for external gifts, were more Jewish than Christian; and, had the matter ended thus, there would have been a danger that religion should become a mere business of belonging to the legitimate assembly and of almsgiving—a danger vastly increased when Christianity became the State religion and the prophetic conception of the holy remnant, the servant of the Lord, gave place to a mixed society which was no longer the leaven, but only had the leaven in it. Then the old real basis of the sacrament as simply the fullest expression of the Christian society was lost.

Not to save the gospel, as Loisy maintains,*

* "The Gospel and the Church," p. 150. "The Church can fairly say that in order to be at all times what Jesus desired the society of His friends to be, it had to become what it has become; for it has become what it had to be, to save the gospel by saving itself."

but because of inability to receive the gospel in its purity, was the Church with its sacrifice of the mass required. A hierarchical priesthood, because it destroyed the original meaning of the broken body and shed blood as victory over that very sense of the might of visible things to which all hierarchical power appeals, could only in that material way express the essential content of Christianity as a religion of pardon and grace. In the materialism of the idea and its departure from the freedom and spirituality of the gospel we should see the very necessity whence it arose. It ignored the royal priesthood of God's children and it reintroduced the law as a schoolmaster, but the leaven of Christianity as a religion of God's pardoning love, as of God's working and not merely of man's winning, continued by it active in the world.

Nevertheless, though it may have been a higher law, the essence of Catholicism is the reintroduction of the law. However much the association of the bishop with the sacraments may have conferred on him mystic and even magical authority, and so prepared the popular mind for his authority in matters of faith, his first claim to be among his presbyters as Peter among the apostles was not to guarantee a sacerdotal but a doctrinal tradition. Against Gnosticism it was determined that he had a *charisma veritatis* by right of succeeding through succession in office to the promise to Peter that he should be the foundation of the Church, and that his faith, interpreted as right doctrine, should not fail.* This interpretation of faith is as important as the reference of it to Peter, for it is only faith interpreted as acceptance of right doctrine which a traditional, external, authoritative guarantee could succour. A living faith which realises that all things work together for good could only rest on finding the Spirit of God's Son in one's own heart, crying "Abba, Father." God's salvation is the basis of such knowledge of God, it being the essence of such knowledge that it is prophetic.

But in the very effort to make it available for a larger circle on easier terms, the true relations begin to be lost, and, in some degree at least, inevitably.

* As the historical significance of a text is not what it means but what it is taken to mean, Matt. xvi. 18 was an important *sedes doctrinae* for the whole development.

Dogmas may be divided into three grades. The first springs directly from the religious experience of the community. Such are the doctrines of the Fatherhood of God, the religious significance of Jesus Christ, the belief in the Spirit of God active in the individual and the community, as in the Apostolic Blessing and the first form of the Apostles' Creed. That can speak only to definitely religious souls.

A doctrine of the second grade seeks intellectual justification and harmony for the former. It would express them in consistent and complete formulæ. The most important instance is the later Trinitarian formula. Mainly it was an attempt, through the doctrine of the *Logos*, made familiar by Greek philosophy, to show that, as the Apologists contended, the common Christian man has a better philosophy than the philosophers and to interpret in their own language Christianity to the Greek thinkers. The exact result was deeply influenced by the Greek spirit, and especially by its faith in intellectual solutions, but anywhere and in any age a religion would be required to appeal to the thinking of its age and even to the spirit of it. Yet, just where the necessity lay, there also was the danger. It was possible to forget that Christianity was a higher knowledge of God precisely because it was not concerned about knowledge at all, but about God's rule, precisely because it was not philosophic but prophetic. The systematised explanation took the place of the religious experience, and with that the common man with his experience of the common life was deposed from being a religious authority, and the instructed man took his place. Yet, even so, it could speak only to people at least intellectually in earnest.

Then a third grade of dogma arises.* It is wanted as a basis for the second, and is the more necessary the more the original basis is forgotten. It is always a doctrine of the Church made authoritative by possessing an authoritative guarantee of the original experience either in a secure tradition, or an inspired Scripture, or an infallible channel of truth. Such an authority can even guarantee mysteries which may be imperative for salvation, but which have nothing to do with God's

* Several writers speak of dogmas of the second grade, but the suggestion of a dogma of the third grade comes from Höffding, "Philosophy of Religion," p. 203.

rule through meekness and lowliness of heart in the common tasks and common sufferings. The common life is apt to lose its religious meaning, so that earnest souls are led to look for God's meaning in a life of special ascetic devotion. Then the evil is confirmed because men lose a sense of the very life for which the liberty of God's children is a requisite. But on the other hand, this grade of dogma can speak to all who will listen, requiring only submission. So Catholicism as an externally guaranteed knowledge of God, necessary for an externally conferred salvation, can be established.*

Yet it is not right to speak of Catholicism as if it were a sad accident, or as if mankind could have done without its discipline. If we

* Catholicism, Sohm says, arises from the desire of the natural man to make religion external. It is the natural religion of the natural man. But the natural man is precisely the problem of every redeeming idea and influence which has ever entered the world. Judaism, Islam, Buddhism, all higher religions, as Harnack says, have passed through a similar stage, setting up a legally fixed tradition as a divine ecclesiastical order. Even orthodox Protestantism has not escaped. "Not priests impose it on the guileless laity, but the laity create the authoritative priests and the ecclesiastical Church order."—"Entstehung u. Entwickelung der Kirchenverfassung u. des Kirchenrechts," 1910, pp. 176–77.

are to speak of failure at all, it ought only to be of man's failure to receive the Christian view of God and of salvation in their fullness and in their mutual dependence.

The changes wrought in the heathen conception of God and the transformation of the whole view of the religious life were so vast and so conspicuous that every Christian apologist could appeal to them in face of the most hostile audience. Under polytheism life had been an incalculable anarchy of terrors. Earth and air were crowded with evil spirits, crying everything except "Abba, Father." All things never wrought together for anything, and least of all for good. To the Christian the sole sovereignty belonged to God, and for His children and for His purpose it wrought for good even in life's worst calamities and hardest duties. This was no mere abstract idea of the unity of the Deity, but the assurance that all life could be put in spiritual subjection and made subservient to one moral task. Nor was it, as with us, a calm assumption. It was a new and revolutionary discovery, which made reconciliation with God a reality of peace, in meekness, patience, and love of the brethren.

On the other hand, no movement in history

has ever escaped all the limitations of the system against which it was a reaction. Though the Early Church was essentially Pauline in the sense that it was Gentile and gave itself no concern about Jewish ritual, it was not Pauline in the sense of being able to understand the whole freedom of Paul's gospel. Judaistic Christianity made up only a small proportion of it, and all direct influence from Judaism, except indeed through the Old Testament, ceased with the fall of Jerusalem. Yet, for the very reason that the Gentile Church had not had the benefit of the Jewish preparation, it developed a Judaic type. In the Apostolic Fathers what has been called a Christian legalism already appears. Even Paul's own expressions want the fullness of Paul's meaning. Justification is God's approval on an obedience which will save us from being condemned with the wicked. Nowhere do we find Paul's triumphant sense of the Father of our Lord Jesus Christ who is mightier than all sin and evil, who works spiritual deliverance through relating us directly to Himself and His rule of love in Jesus Christ. If the apocalyptic hope continues, it is apt to be material and millenarian, without meaning for the individual the joy and peace of knowing that God's rule is at hand and no might of evil can keep it out. Even the sense of the sole monarchy of God has not escaped some influence from the old pagan fear of evil, and men are not able to believe that God can be so near or His rule so triumphant. Only by the strong hand, they think, can He vanquish evil. Something of this naturally reflected itself in the Church, in face of the opposition and criticism of a hostile heathenism. Moreover, simple and material ideas of the power of evil demons continued, and led men to look for material ways of escaping their malignant assaults.*

* In the eucharistic prayer in the "Didaché," knowledge and faith and immortality are made known through Jesus, God's Son, but one is not to come to the eucharist unless he is holy. This condition is understood in a purely moralistic way (x.). "If thou art able to bear the whole yoke of the Lord, thou wilt be perfect; but if thou art not able, what thou art able that do" (vi.). In 1 Clement the very purpose for which the Evangelical references are introduced—submission to the presbyters—marks the difference. The Old Testament is abundantly quoted, but only for its examples of simple obedience. Abraham is faithful, inasmuch as he rendered obedience to the words of God (x.). Peace is the gift of God (xix.), but its pattern is the heavens revolving under His government (xx.) and the moral is obedience to the elders. Love is no longer "all ye are brethren," but endure anything from

If this lowering of Christianity is already apparent in those who were so close to their apostolic teachers, and at a time when men could only have been attracted to Christianity by feeling its power, what wonder if the influence of paganism upon it increased, as it gained position and popularity and became a religion of kings and won the people in masses, often on a merely nominal conversion? The idea of the one God was still mighty, but it was rather as sovereign potentate than Father, and the idea of salvation, though still far above heathenism in spiritual power and moral elevation, was closely associated with ideas of deliverance from demons in this life and from a material hell in the life to come. For so material a salvation men naturally expected the Church to provide material guarantees.

This is said to be a depressing view of the failure of Christianity from the beginning. Even were it so, it would be no answer. There are many depressing things in history which, nevertheless, are true. Yet it would surely be

officials appointed by God in an orderly way (xlii.). The idea of the outward impressiveness of a well ruled institution in face of heathenism is a prominent part of the appeal.

a much more depressing view that Christianity had power for three hundred years to retain its perfection, then lost it, and never was so far from perfection as to-day. What took place was a victory amazing both in its depth and in its extent, but not one emancipated from all historical conditions or one which brought to an end the meaning of history as an unceasing struggle after the only final order, God's rule of love; or, to sum it all up, one which enabled men uniformly to walk by faith and not by sight.

Why, for example, should the spread of Christianity in the Gentile world in the first century have been different from the spread of Christianity in China to-day? Even though the teaching of missionaries who hold quite different views is continued for more than one generation in China, the idea of God is more Jewish than Christian, just as in the Early Church. He is mainly ruler and judge, and Jesus is primarily a Saviour from hell into the bliss of heaven. The teaching is received in a simple, traditional way, and there is a strong tendency to give the same authority to the form as to the substance. Yet with this goes an amazing power to conquer heathen vices, stir unknown depths of tenderness and humility, and to create love to the brethren.*

The philosophy of it, moreover, is as simple as the facts. From the beginning every Christian is under the power of the Spirit of God, but, for the fullness of this possession, there must everywhere be a fullness of the time. As Judaism had prepared the seed-bed, a long discipline of the law must also prepare the field. The fellowship of believers, founded on Christ, governed only by love, and nourished by interchange of spiritual gifts and turning all office into humble service, was realised for a moment at the beginning, and has wrought as leaven in the Church ever since, but it has been as leaven hidden in a great mass of purely human and even pagan belief and custom. Perfection at the beginning can be no more than an inspiration, and unity no more than a brotherhood as yet untouched by the forces that divide. The true perfection and the true unity were not the starting-point. They are the goal, and the rigid systems men

* "The Heathen Heart," by Campbell N. Moody, 1907. A valuable document for the study of Post-Apostolic Christianity.

have held to be perfection have often needed to be broken up by doubt and the hard material bonds they have taken to be unity by division, that we may strive for naught less than God's own truth and the unity of love.

Catholicism thus entered the Church with the first Gentile converts, and was completed by the large masses who joined the great State Church without being converted at all. Then it could appeal with more confidence to its size than to its spirit as the proof of God's approval, and was far away from the society in which the last was first, no one called Rabbi, and Christ alone teacher.

Yet great as the change is, it is not to be sought in mere ideas about the Church. Its source was inability to receive the Father's rule as the believer's sole environment, thoughts of God in which pagan elements mingled with Christian, ideas of salvation in which "spiritual" and "holy" had pagan associations bordering on the material. That was the reason why it was necessary men should again be put under the discipline of law and ceremony which the Catholic Church provided.

As soon as the fellowship of saints was

changed into the mixed society of the Catholic Church, no other result was possible, and the only question remaining is, whether that result could have been avoided. Would it, for example, have been secured by the triumph of Montanism? In the central position Montanism gave to spiritual gifts and not to office, it unquestionably maintained an original element of Christianity. But spiritual elements can only be maintained profitably on spiritual grounds, and in its conception of God and of salvation, Montanism was as external as Catholicism, and probably more legal.

True Christianity is puritanical in the sense of holding the Church to be holy because it is a community of holy persons, but that does not mean persons of visibly moral lives or even of a measure of moral attainment, but people willing to be under the influence of God's Spirit. Hence all puritanism is not Christian, but only that puritanism which would keep itself pure solely by seeking to have more and more of the spirit of love. The failure became still more manifest in Donatism, which was a deliberate attempt to restore, in another way than by the prophetic spirit, the Church to being the holy remnant. It could only proceed by a discipline which dealt with external actions whereby it would have shut the door on the publican and harlot, ceased to be an embodiment of the gospel and become a superficial and hard Phariseeism. Against a worldly rule which could be made quite agreeable to worldly people such protests as Montanism and Donatism were in place, but as they were not able to restore Christianity to a true spiritual faith, they could not restore to it a true spiritual fellowship. A legal puritanism was in place against a legal worldliness in the Church, but it could be no more than a protest, for Catholicism had a place for the penitent, and exalted the mercy of God, which, material as its embodiment was, was more like Christ than pulling up, not by love but by law, the tares whatever might happen to the wheat.

Not our pattern but our standing problem, not the goal of history but its task, was set by the Old Catholicism. The whole problem of our divisions was inevitably appointed when the Church absorbed so rapidly, and so much merely by visible institutions, the vast masses of the pagan world, whose first desire was not to serve in the kingdom of heaven ever present in joy and peace, but somehow to arrive at a heaven wholly beyond our mortal life.

"*HOLY*" *AND* "*CATHOLIC.*"

Kattenbusch, in his discussion of the historical meaning of the Apostles' Creed, deals fully with the terms "holy" and "catholic" as applied to the Church. The history of the words involves the whole relation of the Church to dogma and the means of grace. In its original form, he holds the Apostles' Creed to have been the baptismal confession of the early Roman Church from about 100 A.D. onwards. It was a personal confession, though given in public, the essence of it being the acknowledgment of Jesus as Lord. The effect of the various changes to which it was afterwards subjected was to make it a church creed guaranteeing right doctrine. That is the first great change. The Church is transformed from being a brotherhood of saints, who are one because of a faith which is also a life, into a school in which any man can be guaranteed against error in doctrine.

In the early form the article on the Church is simply *ἁγίαν ἐκκλησίαν*. This he takes to mean an earthly community of the heavenly city. It follows *εἰς πνεῦμα ἅγιον*, a Holy Spirit, meaning practically a Spirit of God. A holy Church in the same way means a Church essentially connected with heaven, the Eternal World, the Spirit, God Himself. In the meaning of "holy" two streams unite. First, there is the New Testament conception that to be of God and to be morally holy are one. The word holy there, too, means of God, but the essence of the gospel is that God's might means regeneration, so that the religious and the moral requirements are both united in love. Second, there is the heathen idea that what is holy is something mysteriously divine, not to be questioned, but to be approached with awe. It is in essence a mystery. For Jesus too the guiding idea was the heavenly, but there was no subordination of the miraculous and the ethical, one to the other, in His conception of God and His kingdom "in heaven." The good is miraculous (Matt. xix. 26), and all God does or establishes is itself a good, or to bring the good into being. Heaven is first a religious conception, but it is in the same breath an ethical. When that identification passes into the background, "holy" becomes a naturalistic conception, however sublimely conceived. As the heathen element in the idea preponderated, the whole empirical manifestation of the Church came to be regarded as the direct creation of the Spirit, as miraculous, mysterious, heavenly magnitudes. That this conception should manifest itself very early is, therefore, not strange, as it entered with the earliest Gentile converts. Both elements persisted in the Church, but the Church came to be related in the first place to the wonderful, and only in the second to the ethical.

Not till many centuries after, the time being a matter still in dispute, was the clause in the Apostles' Creed expanded into *sanctam ecclesiam catholicam*. To this was further added *sanctorum communionem*. In the earliest references this latter expression is expounded both as communion in sacred things and as communion with the saints in the mediæval sense of saints. Probably the former meaning is the original, the Catholic Church being the one possessor of the true sacrament. Catholic comes from καθ' ὅλου. The first known use of the word in connection with Church is in Ignatius ("Smyrn.," viii. 2), "Wheresoever the bishop may appear, there let the multitude (τὸ πλῆθος) be; since, wherever Jesus Christ may be, there is the catholic Church." Here it means the Church in its wholeness, as in the old idea that the Church is complete with the two or three assembled with Christ; though God in Christ is only present now in His representative the bishop. In the dedication of the Martyrdom of Polycarp it means the universal Church, but only in the religious sense of being designed for all, accessible by faith to all. In viii. 1 Polycarp makes mention in prayer πάσης τῆς κατὰ τὴν οἰκουμένην καθολικῆς ἐκκλησίας, meaning the Church in all the world and for all the world. Irenæus speaks repeatedly of a Church which is everywhere, but he does not use the expression catholic for it, probably because the word still carried the older meaning. Had the universal sense originally been empirical, international, the expression doubtless would have been ἡ οἰκουμενικὴ ἐκκλησία, but the deeper religious sense sank into the empirical. As the Church consciousness became external, resting itself on empirical possessions, traditions, and such like, it made the expression Catholic Church official. In Cyprian the Catholic Church is the empirical Great Church, and the ideas Roman and Catholic tend already to coincide ("Das Apostol. Symbol," ii. pp. 691–702).

THE ORTHODOX EASTERN CHURCH

CHAPTER V

THE ORTHODOX EASTERN CHURCH

BEFORE the division between East and West, the Catholic Church meant the Great Church which, in contrast with the Gnostic sects, was throughout the whole Græco-Roman world one, by possessing one rule of faith, one canon of Scripture, and one episcopal teaching and priestly office. The schism left two parties to divide the seamless garment. Yet the Eastern Church does not claim to be Catholic in the same sense as the Roman. By calling itself Catholic the Roman Church makes an exclusive claim. Rome is not a local delimitation as Eastern and Anglican are, but the centre of a claim to universal rule. The Eastern Church only claims to be the Church of the Eastern Empire. Œcumenical patriarch is not universal patriarch, but patriarch of the Empire. The name Anatolian is a relic of the time when to hold by the emperor and his patriarch was to be a Christian.* Hence its characteristic mark is not catholicism, but orthodoxy.

From the seventh century the Eastern Church was ritual and conventional, the Western juristic and political; and from that time onwards the separation was growing, though it was only made final by mutual anathema in the eleventh century. The root of the difference must, however, be sought not in the seventh, but in the beginning of the fourth century, when different conceptions of salvation began to operate. To understand the Eastern Church we must begin with Athanasius.

Möhler objects to Protestantism that every sect in it has a personal founder by whose name it is called.† But the Eastern Church is the Church of Athanasius and the Western of Augustine, in the same sense and for the same reason as the Protestant is of Luther. All alike were reformers, men who recalled the Church to its religious task, and who, by a deeper personal experience of the gospel, gave men a better understanding of what that task

* Kattenbusch, "Confessionskunde," p. 113.

† "Symbolik," ed. 5, p. 7.

is. The objection is not to having founders, but to building on them slavishly, and so missing the inspiration which made them create and renovate.

At the beginning of the fourth century theology was concerning itself mainly about speculations regarding the *Logos*, not as a religious, but as a cosmological idea. The Logos had nothing to do with the Jesus who was among us as one who serves, but was simply a mediating idea between a God untouched by change and a created world immersed in corruption. The Church was thereby in danger of becoming a mere school of philosophy. Athanasius rediscovered neither the man Christ Jesus, nor the God and Father of our Lord Jesus Christ, nor the moral freedom of the gospel, nor its ideas of pardon and grace. He still remained in the circle of ideas compounded of Christianity and Greek philosophy. Yet he interpreted the Logos, not by cosmology, but by man's salvation, and so preserved the Church as a saving institution.

The most important document for understanding the Eastern Church is his treatise on the Incarnation of the Word.* The whole

* περὶ ἐνανθρωπήσεως τοῦ λόγου.

Greek doctrine of salvation is summed up in his phrase, Christ became man that we might be made divine.* It is not, however, a new creation, but a restoration. All creation is subject to corruption, but to man a portion of the Logos was given as a germ whereby he could become wholly divine. Through neglecting the contemplation of God and devising evil, man fell into the general corruption of created things. This physical hold was farther increased by a legal claim, for God had decreed that death should follow sin. God was then in a dilemma between failing in His creation or failing in His word, and mere repentance could neither save His honour nor reverse man's corruption. The Logos by whom man had been made, had, therefore, to take a body which could die to satisfy the law, and live again to quicken men "by appropriation of His body and by the grace of His resurrection." Yet, while He was thus walking as man, He was also as the Logos quickening all things and as the Son dwelling with the Father.

In accordance with Neo-platonic ideas, the Logos is the diffused reason of God. The incarnation means simply His sacramental presence

* *ἀυτὸς γὰρ ἐνηνθρώπησεν ἵνα ἡμεῖς θεωποιηθῶμεν.*

in our humanity. It is a symbol which is also a reality. The life and teaching of Jesus are accorded no significance, for it is not by what He did or said, but by what He is that He saves. The miracles alone which prove Him the creative, sustaining Spirit have religious value, just because He is for Athanasius a sacramental not an ethical incarnation. In the crucifixion everything is symbol, which is also reality. Christ's body is kept undivided, that there might be no pretext to divide the Church; His hands were stretched out, one to draw the Jew and the other the Gentile; He suffered in the air where fallen spirits dwell, to purify the way back to heaven. By this sacrament in our humanity death is vanquished, and absence of the fear of death becomes the supreme evidence of Christianity. Ethical power is mentioned, but only as a mysterious conquest over gross vices. The sting of death is not sin, as Paul understood it, but the loss from our nature of the Divine, immortal substance. Hence redemption is rather to be described as physical than as ethical.

Nor is there any necessary connection between this incarnation and a knowledge of God, except of the most external kind. Christ and the Church incarnate only a sacramental symbol of God, not the reality and might of His endless love as man's goal and also his way.

What salvation is is nowhere set forth. But God needs nothing, sets no task for the world's good, and can be found by each apart. Hence salvation can only be deliverance from corruption (φθορά) into contemplation of God (θεωρία τοῦ θεοῦ). Through it all the vague pantheism of Neo-platonism makes itself felt.

The sensuous element in the Greek also appears. "Man's only relation to God is contemplation, which is not fellowship but enjoyment. . . . The idea of salvation is strongly eudæmonistic, not precisely in the material, but in the æsthetic sense." *

A Church based on such conceptions must primarily be an institution to guarantee orthodoxy and administer mysteries. In the "Catechism of Philaret" the Church is defined as "a divinely instituted community of men, united by the orthodox faith, the law of God, the hierarchy, and the sacraments." †

In the "Orthodox Confession" faith is pri-

* F. Kattenbusch, "Confessionskunde," i. p. 287 ff.

† Schaff, "Creeds of the Greek and Latin Churches," p. 483.

marily faith in the Triune God; but "all articles of the faith which the Catholic and Orthodox Church believes were handed down from our Lord Jesus Christ by the apostles of the Church, and have been expounded and confirmed by the œcumenical councils." * The seven councils were inspired. The Constantinopolitan Creed sums up all essential truth. To guard it intact is to be free from everlasting woe and enter Christ's everlasting kingdom. That anything might exist in Scripture contrary to the councils is undreamt of, for both were in every jot and tittle inspired.

This purely traditional position was made still more paralysing to the intellect by the compromise on the Monophysite question forced on the East by Rome. Monophysitism was the only logical expression of a doctrine of salvation which regarded man as potentially divine, and the incarnation as the presence of God in our humanity for its deification. When another theory was accepted, it could only be held as the orthodox faith by treating it purely as a form of sound words.†

As soon as the dogmas ceased to have a

* Schaff, *op. cit.* p. 277.

† Harnack, "History of Dogma," iii. 170.

living meaning, their only religious value was their symbolical and material efficacy in the rites. There are seven chief mysteries, but the chiefest is the performance of the eucharist, especially by the bishop. There, every gesture, every detail of dress is symbolical and is magically efficacious. This symbolical, magical religion has its most complete and also its most superstitious embodiment in the sacred pictures which are supposed to be actual portraits, giving in some way actual possession of the originals.

A mysterious, natural force, having nothing to do with personal worth, endows the priest for administering the mysteries. The higher orders have a higher power, their gradation being, not hierarchical, as with Rome, but hierurgical.

For this Church it was easy to be, as no other Church has ever been, the State Church, and at the same time non-political. The emperor also might have his mystic endowment, and in any case it mattered little who appointed officers whose holiness consisted, not in personal qualities, but in a sacred rite and a sacred dress; while a Church that has no task to accomplish for the world, except to work on individuals by its rites, has no temptation to aim at political power. Nor is the Eastern Church tempted to subject her laity to supervision as Rome does, seeing that no active moral conditions are needed to benefit by her ministrations.

In short, the institution as it stands is still taken in a wholly uncritical way. The Eastern Church has changed nothing and created nothing, because it has questioned nothing, for centuries. Yet, even so, it has not stood still, for, as Kattenbusch puts it, though it continues to wear a child's face, it is now the wizened child's face of old age. Even the absence of the fear of death in it is less a victory than a defective sense of sin. How, then, can its new birth come, except through intellectual question and anguish of moral struggle?

The Eastern Church has exactly what so many sigh for—a revelation of God as unquestioned as if it were written on the skies, and a priesthood equipped with the sure saving operations. It has never been rent by division; it has hardly been disturbed by difference of opinion. In a sense it has wrought peace, and no doubt it has consoled men and encouraged them and done many mighty works in Christ's name. But what strenuous soul that has inherited the struggle of the West would do anything but abandon his birthright by returning to its fold? And there are signs that Christ is already saying to it, "I came not to bring peace but a sword."

THE ROMAN CATHOLIC CHURCH

CHAPTER VI

THE ROMAN CATHOLIC CHURCH

UNLIKE the Eastern Church, the Roman Catholic has not been able to rest, without question and without theory, on the assurance of its identity with the Church Jesus founded among His apostles. Partly it has been too conscious of change, and partly it claims a rule only a theory of the Church could justify. By degrees this theory has not only become the basis of dogma, but the only ultimate dogma.

The Church is held to be invisible through the presence of God in the Spirit, and visible as founded on Christ's representative. Christ founded it on the visible rock of Peter, and, after the pattern of the Jewish theocracy, created for it an organisation of rulers and powers, dividing it, from the first, into rulers and subjects, hierarchy and people, shepherds and flock.

The Church so constituted is a continuation of the incarnation in Christ's threefold office. As prophetic, it hands on uncorrupted the pure truth revealed by Christ; as high-priestly, it administers the sacrament of the altar and retains and forgives sins; as kingly, it binds and looses on earth what shall be bound and loosed in heaven. Thus equipped, it is Noah's ark in the flood, and *extra ecclesiam nulla salus.* Not to hear it is to be a heathen and public sinner.

Its right to this trust and obedience rests on the endowment of the official order. In all essential details they were appointed by the apostles, who in Scripture always act as plenipotentiaries of Christ and with the infallible power of the Spirit. Disobedience to them was disobedience to the Holy Ghost. As this infallible presence is promised to the end of the world, it must have passed to their successors the bishops, and more particularly the chief bishop, the Pope. Through him, above all, the Spirit infallibly speaks. Without his representative no council is œcumenical, while he can speak without the need of any council. The Church has, thereby, freedom to develop as a living organism without any risk of altering the doctrine of Christ.

This Church manifests the four marks stated in the Constantinopolitan Creed: (1) *Apostolicity.* Its officers are either direct successors of the apostles or have been taken up into the succession by service in the Apostolic Church. Chiefly this succession is displayed in the Roman see, which has kept free from all errors and weathered all storms. (2) *Unity.* Unity of spirit is touched on lightly and stress laid on unity of organisation. Unity resides in the bishops who are in union with the Pope. The Eastern schism left the centre, the principle of unity, unimpaired; and how little of it went with Protestantism their chaos of conflicting fellowships declares. (3) *Catholicity.* That means her power to extend herself in the world and continue unshaken in time, and still more to display everywhere and always the same truth, grace, and virtue. (4) *Holiness.* This is not understood in the Puritan sense, which is repudiated, but in the sense that the Church possesses the means of making holy, succeeds with some of her members, and is a sphere marked off from the crowd of heathen and sinners for all. "The Church has the full, unadulterated water of eternal life, and, with her crown of the seven sacraments, sanctifies the whole life of the Christian from the cradle to the grave." *

From this conception it is manifest that the fundamental difference between the Western and the Eastern Church is that, while the latter is primarily a hierurgical saving institution, the former is primarily a hierarchical.

The history of a hierarchical society is manifestly of more importance for understanding it than that of a hierurgical, for authority can never be adequately defended in theory till it is first won in fact.

In the second half of the second century the theory that the bishop among the presbyters was Peter among the apostles first arose. In all likelihood it originated in Rome itself. But every bishop was still a successor of Peter. As the direct successor of Peter, the Roman bishop gained a place of pre-eminence from the theory, but, as each bishop was Peter, all had "the Roman episcopate." All, as Cyprian says, are pastors of the one flock, each represents the whole *ecclesia*. The theory, therefore, afforded no ground for a primacy.

By the beginning of the third century the

* Article "Kirche" in "Wetzer und Weltes Kirchen-lexicon," by Paul Schanz.

bishop, who had hitherto only been the religious head, had become the ecclesiastical head of the community. But, though his *charisma* was now official, the memory of the days when its exercise depended on recognition by the congregation still appeared in this, that his acts were not valid without the representatives of the community. The prominence of the bishop of Rome was still due only to the prominence of the imperial city with its unique associations.

During the course of the third century the churches of the great cities, especially of Rome, Alexandria, and Antioch, came into prominence through the rapid extension of a Christianity which they alone were in a position to aid and which was accepted as Catholic on their recognition. Further, the acquisition of great buildings and property and the general rapid growth in numbers between the Decian and Valerian persecutions favoured ecclesiastical more than spiritual development.

Matters of discipline were decided as before by the congregation through its representatives. But questions arose which affected larger areas, and then the bishops of other communities were invited to consult. So the provincial synod grew up. Backed by the pre-eminence of his own community, the Bishop of Rome became supreme in his provincial synod, and by the end of the third century could through it depose other bishops and put his own nominees in their places.

The recognition of Christianity as the State religion at the beginning of the fourth century led the Council of Nicæa to model the ecclesiastical organisation on the imperial. Each provincial capital had a metropolitan with dependent bishops. Rome was thereby strengthened by being accorded the first place, but it was also weakened by the recognition of formidable rivals.

The œcumenical council, moreover, was a creation of the Emperor, not the Pope. The Emperor summoned it, confirmed its decrees, and dissolved it. From Nicæa onwards an imperialism centring in the Emperor and an imperialism centring in the Pope, an imperialism of the new Rome and of the old were in conflict. In spite of the prestige of the ancient seat of empire, the Emperor was able by means of the œcumenical council to break the power of Rome in the East, and, even in the West, the triumph of the papacy was only secured by the incoming of the barbarians and the fall of the Western Empire.

By this invasion of the barbarians the development of Roman Catholicism through the Middle Ages and down to our own time has been largely determined. It brought to an end constitutional ideas and afforded scope for personal rule, and it provided a wholly uncultured people who received Christianity implicitly on authority. Thus the authoritative and disciplinary character of the Church was determined by the needs of these simple and rude peoples. Furthermore, the founding of Arian German kingdoms drove the Catholics everywhere into the arms of the Pope, their sole protector.

When general councils again appeared in the West, they were not the old œcumenical councils, but were an extension of the Roman provincial synod, of which the Pope from the first was head and by which he became head of Western Christendom.

Without seeking to clothe error in the robe of historical necessity, it can be seen that the Western Church was a great advance upon the Eastern as a discipline for the gospel, and even as a realisation of it.

The difference lay in the practical and juridical temper of the Roman Church. Such a temper is concerned with sin, not merely with corruption. Its problem is universal sinfulness, not merely universal mortality. Its salvation is not merely an infused divine life, but a life meriting the approval of God as judge. Jesus does not so utterly disappear into a philosophical abstraction, but, being legal mediator between God and man, His human is as essential as His divine nature to His work. Through penance on the basis of works and merit, His "satisfaction" became prominent, and so, externally but sincerely, the cross was preached, and, however legally conceived, Christianity was presented as a religion of reconciliation.

Nevertheless, the temper of the Roman Church is primarily legal. Nothing shows this more clearly than the continuance of penance, which had disappeared in the Eastern Church except as a form. At first it existed in its ancient severity, and then in the milder form of the confessional. It rests upon the idea of God as sovereign potentate and of pardon as State condonation. As this naturally does not operate till the culprit has done his best, the question of merit is inextricably mixed up with the question of pardon. The necessity of measuring men's sins by rule, which the confessional imposes, still further fixed reconciliation in a legal framework. It turned God into a Father Confessor and salvation into the reward of a calculable merit.

The highest result was the mediæval conception of the Church, the final expression of which is found in Thomas Aquinas. The evangelical ideas are not lost. The Church is the body of Christ, and from Him grace flows to all the members. But the evangelical element is entirely subordinated to the hierarchical. The sacraments are the channels of grace, and the priest is necessary to the sacraments, and, from the idea of a body, it is argued that a visible head is necessary to the priest. The Pope is necessary to the Church's unity.* Especially he must keep her one. To that end Christ prayed for Peter that his faith fail not, and all his successors are similarly guarded.† Moreover, the Pope has power in the Church, as a king has in the State, to give plenary indulgence at his will.‡ Finally, as spiritual goods are above

* "Summa": Secunda secundae, quaest., 40. art. 6.

† Ibid. 1. art. 10.

‡ Tertia, supp. quaest., 26. art. 3.

earthly, the successor of Peter, the Vicar of Christ, is above all princes, and may at once claim their service and dispose of their lot. When, after giving heretics a chance of repentance, he or his representatives—and the whole priesthood are now only his representatives—excommunicate them, the secular arm to which they are handed over must exterminate them; * and if it be the prince himself who is excommunicated, his subjects are set free from their allegiance.†

That was the amazing outcome of the idea of God as a potentate ruling by a visible plenipotentiary and of pardon as State condonation.

The immense power of such an institution for the disciplining of the barbarous peoples is beyond question. But already in the twelfth and thirteenth centuries, when, through the fulfilment of this task, Rome had reached the height of her glory, she was insisting on a guardianship after she had trained her children to pass beyond it.

Now, pupilage is one thing and what Kant calls heteronomy is another. The mere pro-

* Secunda secundae, quaest., 11. art. 3.

† Ibid., quaest., 12. art. 2.

duction of the idea of works of supererogation seems to speak of a total failure to awake the deeper and finer judgment of the conscience. The necessity of appraising virtue and vice by rule, which the confessional imposes upon the priest, produces a vast system of casuistry which must often do more to provide excuses than to search the heart. But the deeper evil is that the moral judgment which could be our own and is not, which we accept from another when we might have it from our own consciences, is, by that very fact, corrupt. Hence, as Loofs says, "Rome remains the mother of obedient children, but to religious and moral independence she cannot educate them. Where moral independence exists, it has come to pass not through the Church's training, but in spite of it." *

The consequence is that, though she has still room for much noble piety, those who revolt from her authoritative traditional guidance seem to be left morally and spiritually bankrupt, while great masses of those she retains are still allowed to cherish superstitious, pagan, and purely naturalistic views of religious succour. And both follow, if God is the moral

* "Symbolik," i. 387.

potentate whose salvation is endangered by nothing so much as moral independence.

The only answer has been to insist on still further tutelage. When the councils which had helped the Pope to power threatened to become his rivals, the moment when the forces of opposition were weakened by the Reformation was seized upon to produce one more council to bring the power of councils to an end.

When the councils passed, the practical temper of the Roman Church did not suffer it to be enslaved to the past as the Eastern Church had been. It wished to exalt tradition, but had no mind to be hampered by it, so it fell upon the device of an infallible guardian of tradition who has infallible power to adapt it. Reversing the Apostle's idea of being set free with freedom, it obtained liberty of action by autocracy, the Vatican Decree of 1870 making the Pope the sole instance in doctrine and in government. Then, as Sohm expresses it, Catholic Christianity offered up on the altar of the papacy its Christian freedom which had once rested on the conviction that in every believing Christian the Spirit of God was active.*

* "Kirchenrecht," i. 455.

AUGUSTINE

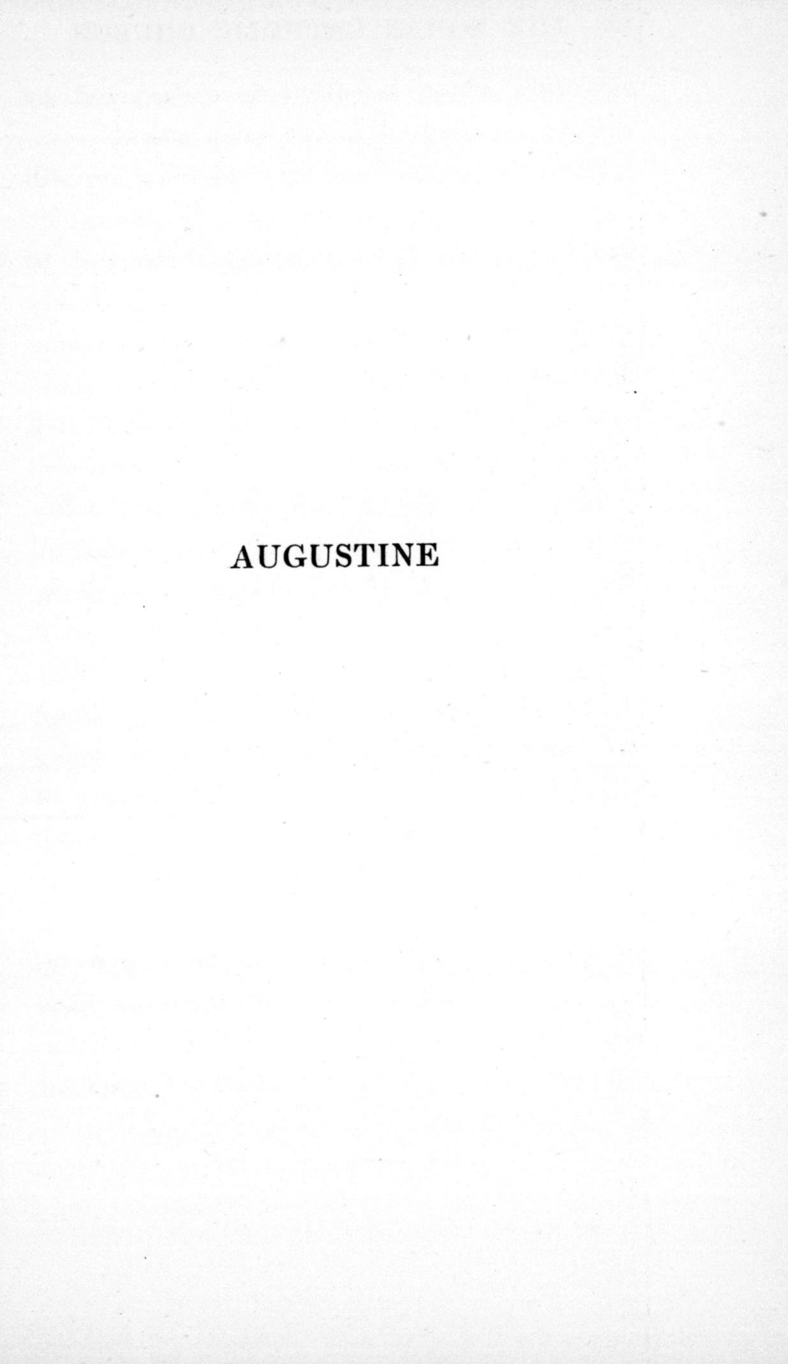

CHAPTER VII

AUGUSTINE

THE difference between the Eastern and the Western Church is largely a matter of race. Apparently a legal and juridical temper was characteristic even of the old Roman paganism.* But part of it also was derived from individual teachers, and that is still truer of the higher elements which dwelt in it.

For the external form no one did more than Cyprian. Harnack thus sums up his influence: "He established the rule of the hierarchy in the Church, confirmed episcopalism, naturalised the conceptions of a legal relation between man and God, of works of penance as a means of grace and of the Christian's satisfactory expiatory doings; and already he had

* Mommsen, "History of Rome," Eng. tr., i. 182 (1888).

fashioned clerical speech with its formal pomp, cold-blooded anger, and misapplication of biblical phraseology for the interpretation and criticism of contemporary affairs." *

From the lawyer Tertullian the system borrowed legal language and legal subtleties, and was confirmed in its view of God as a punctilious judge of His rights.

Through Augustine it was enabled to weave the conception of the congregation of saints into the warp of the official Church, so that religious and clerical ideas were indistinguishably mingled in the conception of authority.

The process, which had been going on for two centuries, of substituting the official for the religious order, was thereby completed, yet, through the influence of Tertullian and especially of Augustine, something of the religious order was saved even in the very act of clothing the official order with more power. It was an evil that penitence, pardon, grace, love should have their security through the hierarchy and not through the Spirit of God, but it was good that they remained, even in that imperfect way, active in the Church.

In Tertullian there was an original and re-

* "History of Dogma," iii. 23; Eng. tr., v. 25.

ligious spirit which saved the Church from the view that the significance of grace ended with baptism, and that thereafter man's sole relation to God was watchfulness not to offend Him, even though his own puritanism tended to make him think that less should be expected from God on a second occasion after He had pardoned once.

Augustine's work is so vital for understanding the whole inward spirit of the Roman Church and all the conflicting influences which wrought in her and finally rent her asunder, and is, moreover, so vital for understanding the rise of Protestantism, that it will be necessary to consider his teaching in some detail.

The Church had become conscious that she was no longer a community separate from the world. Upon that separation all her earlier convictions had rested. Wherefore, as the prosperous State Church, she required a new view of herself. This Augustine endeavoured to provide for her. He was born in the middle of the fourth century, when Pope Liberius was consciously pursuing the ambition to make the Church a great world power by absorbing the still heathen masses of the people, and he carried on his work through the first third of the fifth, when, in the breaking up of the Empire, the Church remained almost the sole organising power, truly the only ark for civilisation in the submerging flood. To keep the Church at such a time in any way mindful of her religious task was no small merit, and it was no wonder that, in such a time, he made too much of its external embodiment.

We shall begin with his view of the relation of the Church to the civil society on the one hand and to the society of the elect on the other.

The recognition of Christianity as the State religion he took to be the fulfilment of prophecy. The sin of the Donatists is that they divide the Church at this moment of triumph. Nor are they justified by the faults of Catholics. "Abraham believed and all nations are promised to him; has Cæcilianus sinned and are all nations lost?" * The State principle is mere force, but, as the Church helps it to a better principle, the State rightly uses force to help the Church. In particular it rightly represses the Donatists.† Catholics desire that

* "Sermo," 359. 5; v. 1594. (The Roman numerals indicate the vol. in Migne's edition.)

† "C. Lit. Pet.," 2. 203; ix. 324.

the Donatists be saved from the pains of eternal justice by terror of human judgment.* Once Augustine had thought that we should operate only with the word, fight only with argument, vindicate only by reason, preferring open heretics to feigned Catholics: but the practical success of compulsion changed his view.† The Master's mildness was because the prophecy that all kings of the earth shall worship Him had not then been fulfilled. In proportion as it is fulfilled the Church makes more use of power, and not only invites but compels to good.‡ "Compel them to come in" in the parable means compel those in the by-ways of error to enter the sacred unity of the Church. Like other men, kings must serve God with their special endowments as well as with their common human nature. "Now the taking away of idols, so long ago predicted, no private individual could command, human society being what it is. Therefore, kings, by the fact that they are kings, have whereby they may so serve God as those cannot who are not kings."§

* "Ep." 100. ; ii. 366. † "Ep." 93. 5. 17 ; ii. 329.

‡ "Ep." 173. 10 ; ii. 757.

§ "C. Lit. Pet.," 2. 210 ; ix. 330.

Whether the result is persecution or not depends entirely on whether it is for a good cause or a bad.* If by some mistake the good suffer, it is justified as evil is under God's government, by the power of the good to make profitable use of their afflictions.†

Here we have the foundation of the Roman doctrine of the prince as the defender of the faith and of the Protestant view of him as the guardian of the two tables of the law, views which, possibly more than anything else, helped to obscure the true nature of the Christian society.

On the other hand, the State, apart from what it derives from the Church and the services it can render the elect, is no divine society, but the use of force, mainly in the service of the lust of rule.‡ Even the nominally Christian Roman State is only the mass who are to perish in the flood, amid which the Church alone is as Noah's ark.§

* "C. Lit. Pet.," 2. 212; ix. 332.

† "Ep." 105. 2. 7; ii. 398. "The State is the earthly providence. . . . As God can impose sufferings for trial and progress, so may the State. If anything does, this reminds us of the Roman element in Augustine" (H. Schmidt, "Des Augustinus Lehre u. die Kirche," Jahrbücher f. deut. Theol. vi. 254).

‡ "De Civ.," 5. 12; vii. 154 ff. § Ibid. 15. 26; vii. 472.

There is still a religious mood in Augustine to which the Roman State is Antichrist, as it was to the older Christianity. The heavenly city may profit by such help as the State affords her, but her true peace she can only possess by faith, and she is often compelled to dissent from the State and suffer at its hands. This is only avoided "in so far as the minds of their enemies have been alarmed by the multitude of Christians and quelled by the manifest protection God affords them."* The State is still steeped in pagan religion; it is the city of the ungodly who do not sacrifice to God alone, and so cannot give the soul its proper command over the body, nor the reason its just authority over the vices, and which, therefore, is void of true justice.† For the most part its inhabitants are of those who do not belong to the city of God, but inherit eternal misery.‡

Here we have the foundation of the mediæval idea of the subordination of the State to the Church which imposed upon the reformers the necessity of finding a juster place for the secular life, and exposed them to a too ready

* "De Civ.," 19. 17; vii. 646.

† Ibid. 19. 24; vii. 656. ‡ Ibid. 19. 28; vii. 658.

acceptance of the State as the basis of religious fellowship.

The relation of the Church to the congregation of the elect is more complex and more important. Some of the most earnest students of Augustine do not find any connection at all.* They find simply an intense practical interest in the Church as it existed, and an intense religious interest in the doctrines of grace, not springing one from the other, nor dependent one upon the other. There is certainly no serious attempt to combine them, and nothing made Augustine so great a ferment in the Church as the fact that down the ages the two tended more and more to work apart and even to conflict. Yet his practical combination of the two ideas was his greatest contribution to the development of mediæval Catholicism.

His view of the Catholic Church is mainly traditional. The tradition is still of the time when the Church was not yet the mixed society it had become. From Cyprian he accepted the view that no salvation was possible outside the Catholic Church, that her bishops were successors of the apostles and *dispensatores dei*, and that the unity of the Church rests upon

* Esp. H. Reuter, "Augustinische Studien," 1887.

the unity of the Episcopate. The unimportant place this view occupies in his writings is due entirely to the fact that all parties accepted it. The Donatists also had this organisation and held this view, and the only question was which was Church and which schism. But there is not yet any theory of the Church's authority, and it seems to be subordinated to Scripture, and though we could not believe without its help, we can be helped to pass beyond authority to knowledge.*

The original ground for the belief in the efficacy of baptism and of salvation within the Church was the vast contrast between the Church and the world. To enter the Church by baptism was a change into a new spiritual realm; to belong to its fellowship was to enter a bond of mutual succour and supplication and to live really in dependence upon Christ. Augustine's view that baptism was efficacious

* *E.g.*, "Yet to the Scriptures alone, without any restriction, I owe assent" ("De Nat. et Grat.," 1. 61. 71; x. 282), compared with other Catholic writings; and "De Civ.," 11. 3; vii. 318. Of course, both Church and Scripture are divine authorities, proved so by being spread throughout the earth ("Conf.," 6. 5. 8; i. 723; 6. 11. 19; i. 729), and therefore agree, so that no subordination is necessary in practice.

not because of the person who administered it, but because it was Christ's own mark,* and that it became effective when the baptized were within the circle of the Church's prayers,† had originally a real basis, a basis, that is, in what the Church actually was. So long as the Church was definitely separate from the pagan world, to enter her communion was to pass into a fellowship of prayer and love which truly meant a new life. His view of the eucharist also, as the offering up of herself by the Church which is His body, through Christ her head,‡ belonged to the time when the theory of a Christian was that his life was a daily offering to God.

But Augustine had to face the situation that in the great State Church that condition of things had definitely come to an end. The Donatist hope of maintaining in prosperity, by human discipline, a Church without spot or wrinkle such as had been maintained by the divine discipline in ages when Christianity had been a persecuted remnant, he could no longer cherish. The Church was a *corpus domini bipar-*

* In Joann. 5. 6; iii. 2015.

† "De Bap.," 3. 17. 22; ix. 149.

‡ In Joann. 26. 15; iii. 1614; Serm. 272; v. 1247; Loofs D. G. 409.

titum, which he interprets as true and mixed and again as true and counterfeit.* But if there were a possibility of some genuine religion being without and a certainty of much of the world being within, the theory of the Church as the only ark of salvation could not escape becoming more ecclesiastical and more artificial.

This appears in the means he takes to deny that Christianity could exist outside the Catholic unity. He reverses the apostolic order, and instead of basing unity on love, he bases love on unity.† While he cannot deny the holy lives and true faith of many Donatists, he can find no motive for their separation but pride.‡ He is thereby enabled to deny that the love which alone makes a true Christian can exist in any of them.

Size becomes the evidence of God's approval, the mark of Catholicity; the chief argument against the Donatists being that they are a miserable minority.§ The result is an absence, in the writings against them, as in nothing

* "De Doc. Chr.," 2. 32 ; iii. 82.

† "De Bap.," 3. 16. 21 ; ix. 149.

‡ 3. 19. 27 ; ix. 152 ; and "C. Corr. Don.," 9. 42 ; ii. 811, no one can be righteous so long as he is separated from the unity of this body.

§ "C. Litt. Pet.," 2. 38. 91 ; ix. 292 ; 2. 32. 74 ; ix. 284.

else he ever wrote, of the very charity of which he speaks and upon which the Apostle had based all true unity. His is a tribal idea of love, which unfortunately neither began with him nor altogether flowed from him. But every resource of his rhetoric he used to give this, that is the denial of the original basis of the Church, the sanction of his great name. The prophetic idea of the holy remnant was definitely set aside for the Church, and was only recovered by the idea of the elect.

Having lost the old real basis for baptism, Augustine produces the artificial view that it leaves an indelible mark like the emperor's mark on a soldier. In a deserter it is without effect, but it remains the reason why the army claims him and why it need not be repeated when he returns.* This naturally led at a later time to the idea of an indelible mark of ordination upon the person who had power to imprint such a sacramental mark, and then the Church, having lost the ground of the old view, was ready for an equally ecclesiastical and artificial view of the eucharist as a rite of priestly not personal sacrifice.

Augustine had inherited the ordinary Catho-

* "Serm.," 359. 5 ; v. 1594.

lic view that there could be no salvation outside the Catholic Church. But though without Church and sacraments none could be saved, with them many might still be lost.* He, therefore, distinguished the true Church as the elect, and the elect were those who would be saved into the bliss of heaven. No elect person will ultimately remain outside the Catholic Church, but hypocrites, though they appear to be in it, are not truly of it. Only those who mourn the evils within her compose the glorious Church without spot or wrinkle.

That might mean that the Church consists of the sincere, but it is election proved by final perseverance, God's gift to His elect, and not present sincerity, which distinguishes the true seed of Abraham who alone are the true Church. From the study of Scripture, he says, he was convinced that he had erred when he thought that the faith by which we believe in God was not God's gift but from ourselves.† "The effect of God's compassion cannot be in man's power that He should have compassion in vain, if man will not; because if He will

* "De Civ.," 1. 35; vii. 46. Only the elect are "redempta familia Domini et peregrina civitas regis Christi."

† "De Praed.," 3. 7; x. 964.

have compassion, He is able to call them in a manner so suited to them that they shall be moved." * The number of the elect exactly supplies the place of the fallen angels, and one cannot be added to the number or taken from it.†

This true Church is so far dependent on the

* "De Div. Quaest.," i. 2. 12–16; vi. 117–21.

† "Neque augendum, neque minuendum." "De Corr. et Grat.," 13. 39; x. 940. This change of opinion has been frequently passed over. Augustine's view is said to be that God gives all men a *sufficing* grace which their good will can render *efficacious*, and that it is a perversion of Jansenius that there is only *efficacious* grace which God gives to some and refuses to others ("Saint Augustine," Ad. Hatzfeld, Eng. tr., 1898, p. 92). His doctrine of election is said to mean merely that we must think of God as foreknowing what men will decide and not as controlling their decision ("S. Austin," W. Cunningham, 1886, p. 89). These statements are only true of his earlier view. According to his later view foreknowledge is not of what men will do, but what He Himself will do ("De Praed.," 18. 36; x. 987). Grace is an *inspiratio bonae voluntatis* by which we begin, continue, and attain ("De Corr. et Grat.," 1. 2. 3; x. 917). God elects not because in the future men are to be holy, but in order that they may be holy ("De Praed.," 18. 36; x. 987). "Ut divina gratia indeclinabiliter et insuperabiliter ageretur ("De Corr. et Grat.," 12. 38; x. 940). No less than Calvin he believes that men are lost simply because God does not elect them, and he only seems to get rid of the difficulty more easily by his shallower and purely negative idea of evil.

Catholic Church that the latter is the sole sphere of the Spirit. Her unity is not the result of the working of the Spirit, but the organ and sole sphere of it, so that any one veritably joined to it receives the Spirit,* but a schismatic who is no drunkard, or idolater, or lascivious, or a lover of money, or given to witchcraft is as certain of perdition as a Catholic who is.† The reason given is that he lacks charity. But that only shows how arbitrary is the idea of charity, a fact which becomes more apparent when it is admitted that he may have faith outside and every Christian gift except this ecclesiastically conditioned charity.‡

On the other hand the Catholic Church is constituted by the elect, and not yet by the bishop. When Parmenius would set the bishop between the people and God, Augustine asks what he makes of the good and faithful Christians and of Christ as an advocate with the Father. All Christians shall mutually commend each other in their prayers, no one

* "C. Cresc.," 2. 13. 16 ; ix. 476; and "De Bap.," 3. 17. 22 ; ix. 149.

† "De Bap.," 4. 18. 25 ; ix. 170.

‡ Ibid., 5. 24. 34 ; ix. 193.

coming between but He who is the true mediator for all. Even Paul, though a chief member, yet, as a member, commends himself to the prayers of the Church and does not make himself a mediator between the people and God, but asks that all the members of the body of Christ should pray one for another.* Yet, as has been said, by the Catholic Church he understood the Church as it was actually organised, and the problem is how he combined these two conceptions of a Church with rulers appointed to govern it, and which derived its unity from the giving of the keys to Peter, with a fellowship which had absolutely no source except the inscrutable election of God.†

For any explanation that may exist besides the acceptance of the current view of his time, we must turn our attention to his conception of God and of salvation.

For both, his view of grace is first in importance. No doubt it was determined mainly by his own conversion. The reality of some intense experience which was the beginning of victory over fleshly lusts is manifest whether we consider the fervour with which he speaks

* "C. Ep. Parm.," 2. 8. 15. 16; ix. 59-60.

† "De. Bap.," 3. 17. 22; ix. 149.

of grace, or the place he assigns to lust as the chief evidence that the body has rebelled against its master the soul and as the vehicle of original sin. The idea that he made a calm transition to philosophical asceticism is neither true to the impression left after all possible deductions have been made from his own writings, nor to human nature. But the Neoplatonic element in his conversion and subsequent struggle he himself makes sufficiently plain.

He stood between God and the phantasmal, the material world, lifted up towards God by beauty but pressed down by carnal habit. Loving God and cohering in Him means abiding in His unity, and he seeks to pass to it by abstraction from the world of sense and by ecstasy. * But this purely intellectual salvation

* "Conf.," 7. 17. 23–24; i. 744 f. There are the usual four stages of Neoplatonic emancipation: (1) "gradatim a corporibus ad sentientem per corpus animam"; (2) "inde ad ejus interiorem vim"; (3) "inde rursus ad ratiocinantem potentiam." Finally, being now withdrawn from "contradicentibus turbis phantasmatum," and dimly feeling the immutable, he reaches reality by a flash of insight in "ictu trepidantis aspectus." The complete Neoplatonism of bk. vii. may be later than his conversion, but that only makes the abiding and possibly the increasing influence of Neoplatonism in his thinking the more apparent.

was too bloodless and too little humble to conquer his strong sensuous nature. That succour he found in Christ, and in a very real and practical way in His humble service. Hence, although at his conversion Augustine seems to have been amazingly ignorant of Christianity, his reading back of more Christian ideas into his conversion than he was at the moment conscious of, is no mistaken interpretation of the forces which made him what he was.

Yet the Neoplatonic idea of God and the Neoplatonic theory of redemption continued to hold him to the end, and through them he interpreted even his Christian experience.*

Neoplatonism was mysticism. To pantheism God is wholly immanent—all is God; to mysticism God is wholly transcendent—God is all. He alone is being, and all else has real existence only so far as it partakes of His substance. This substance is simple, like light, and only turns into the

* "Inseparably the biblical and Neoplatonic elements mingle in him, and although all his later life it was biblical and ecclesiastical Christianity he wished to stand for, the latter continued to restrict the former more than the former the latter" (Loofs, "Dogmengeschichte," p. 410, 1906).

phenomenal world as it is broken up, so to speak, in its descent through the unreality of matter. But the human soul with its centre of unity so partakes of the Divine unity that, by returning into itself, it may escape the sensuous world, rise to pure thought and, then, in an ecstatic vision pass beyond the divisions of thought, see the white undivided light and find the beauty and learn the bliss of being reabsorbed into the undivided unity of God. Thus Greek philosophy, which started out to seek the unity which would embrace all things, ended with the bare unity itself, with absorption in the naked absolute. "In the ascent to the Divine unity the mystic loses hold of everything by which he could characterise it, and, when he arrives at it, it is with naked hands."* Yet it is not difficult to understand the attraction of such a system amid a crumbling civilisation. It helped men to ignore, if not to conquer. It was the best substitute they could find for faith in God's rule in the midst of it, also making God man's sole environment, saying there was nothing but God. Yet it could not say "All

* E. Caird, "The Evolution of Theology in the Greek Philosophers," ii. 215.

things work together for good," and it had nothing to cry in men's hearts, "Abba, Father." Hence it could only teach men to ignore, and not to inherit the earth, and it could only efface, not rescue, the distressed moral personality.

Even in Augustine's most scriptural expressions this mystical idea of God can be detected. God is a truth regarding which, the moment we ask what it is, the darkness of corporeal images and the cloud of phantasms beset us. There is a truth which alone is simple and on that account alone unchangeable, which is God, whereby all goods are created, but not simple and, therefore, not unchangeable.* It is only a human mode of expression to say He is moved at all by our good or ill. When He is said to be angry with the evil and kind to the good, they are changed, not He. Even when we speak of God loving us, nothing happens to the substance itself of God, but only to the creature in respect to which it is said.†

Augustine's imagination of God as a vast lake and of the world as a sponge, through which more or less perfectly it percolates,

* "De Civ.," 11. 10; vii. 325.

† "De Trin.," 5. 16. 17; viii. 924.

continued, in spite of his rejection of its material imagery, to represent his view of God and the world.

In accordance with Christian teaching he held that the world was a creation by God, not an emanation from Him, but the distinction has singularly little effect upon his thought. "Nothing" plays much the same rôle with him as "matter" in the ancient thinking. It is the unformed alien element in which the Divine light is broken up and restricted. Thus he says, "As far as anything is 'nature' God made it, but in so far as it is 'corruptible,' it is 'nothing.'"* Again, all things below God neither wholly are nor wholly are not.† That is to say, they are only real in so far as they partake of the simple substance of God.

Evil belongs to "nothing," not to God. In so far as anything exists it is good.‡ To that nature which is the highest, by whose making all things are, no nature is contrary unless it be what is not.§ This idea that sin is just *privatio boni*, that is absence of God,

* "C. Ep. Man.," § 39 ; viii. 201.

† "Conf.," 7. 11. 17 ; i. 742.

‡ Ibid., 7. 12. 18 ; i. 743.

§ "De Civ.," 12. 2 ; vii. 350.

he is never weary of repeating. The opposite, therefore, must also be plain, that all true being is not merely God's creation but the communication of God Himself.

In accordance with Scripture teaching he holds that the soul is not a part of God but a creation of God.* Moreover, he agreed with the current Christian teaching in finding the origin of sin in freedom. But it is not only Adam's freedom, and far away from practical issues; it is not a blemish in creation at all, as it must have been, were it really a misuse of freedom. All natures have their measure and inward harmony and they are changed into better or worse as the Divine foreknowledge sees good for the scheme of governing the universe.† The things above are better than those below, but all together are better than those above.‡ Therefore, it is not on the ground of man's freedom that God is justified, but on His right to communicate Himself as far as He will, and that, where He is not there is no reality, so that there is nothing evil

* "De Civ.," 7. 5; vii. 199.

† Ibid., 12. 2; vii. 350.

‡ "Conf.," 7. 13. 19; i. 744.

either in God or in His creation. Evil is only the antithesis which adorns the poem of existence, an ornament of God's rhetoric, an eloquence not of word but of things.*

Here we have the radical failure of Augustine's teaching. In his thinking he has little more place for the moral personality than Neoplatonism had, however much more his Christian experience meant for him in feeling. This will appear if we compare his doctrine of election with Paul's. To Paul it is a religious assurance that neither life nor death nor any created thing can separate him from the love of God which is in Christ Jesus his Lord. It sets him in the midst of God's world as God's child. Occasionally Augustine's heart is moved in the same way. "Two things are not doubtful to me—His goodness and my faith." † But his habitual thought is that no one can be sure of having received the gift of perseverance.‡ In so far as his doctrine of election maintained that all goodness is of God's grace, it was a religious idea, but it had not the religious interest that, because

* "De Civ.," 11. 18; vii. 332.

† "Enn. Ps.," 10. 5; iv. 134.

‡ "De Dono Pers.," 1, 1; x. 993.

it is of God, we may rely on it. In the last issue, though he never denied free-will in the philosophical sense, the source of the doctrine was not Paul, but the necessitarian, mystical, pantheistic feeling of Neoplatonism.

This idea of transferring its whole value beyond the grave is significant. Faith in Christ has not its issue in finding rest for our souls now as the foretaste and pledge of the rest which remains. Whether before or after Christ's coming, faith in Him alone leads to God.* But it only avails for those God has predestined to be of the city of God, and that means those who are to have the supreme good, the life eternal.† So exclusively is it measured by the future that no one is to trust that he has passed from death to life till he has reached the place where there is no temptation.‡ Nothing, Augustine says, stirs love like the knowledge that we are loved, but it is not on that kind of appeal that he bases our security in heaven. That rests not on an emancipation but on a suppression of the moral personality. Man's first freedom was to be able not to sin, his

* "De Civ.," 18. 47; vii. 609.

† 19. 4; vii. 627. ‡ 21. 15; vii. 729.

last will be to be unable to sin. But that is a renovation by power, not love; by God overriding our nature, not giving it the victory. So little can he use any idea of freedom that, though he calls this the highest freedom, it is really an assertion that freedom is a mere evil.*

Wherefore, in spite of all he says of penitence, grace, and love, it is not with sin as guilt, but with immersion in material desire as remoteness from God, that salvation is concerned. He finds himself far from God "in the region of dissimilarity,"† far from the highest beauty, the highest good, by being absorbed in the lower beauties, the lower goods. These lower goods are the objects of earthly desire and especially of carnal lust. Sin springs from pride and self-love, but it works by the propagation of desire. Augustine is not without some genuine understanding that this pride and self-love needs to be changed, and that there is some important relation of Christ's humility to it.‡ But, when he comes to think the matter out, God's grace in Jesus Christ is not something to humble our pride and touch our self-love, to

* "De Civ.," 22. 30. 3; vii. 802.

† "Conf.," 7. 10; i. 742. ‡ Ibid., 1. 1; i. 661.

make us realise that our pride rejects God's love and our self-love His fellowship, but is an influx of God's substance into the unreality of our being, the working of which is to withdraw us from the distraction of desire to the unity of an undisturbed contemplation. So it leads to sacramental grace and asceticism.

The doctrine of the Trinity in so far as it is not traditional is a doctrine of how the simple substance of God passes out of itself and returns into itself again, and in so far as it has religious interest it is to assure a similar return for us also into the unity of God. Christ also is interpreted as the *nous* whereby He gives everything form—that is, reality. His incarnation is the manifestation in human life of the one undivided Divine principle.* That principle, and not His flesh nor His human soul, is our purification. Even when we read of "love," we can never be sure that it is more than a name for the Divine substance.† The

* "De Civ.," 10. 24; vii. 301.

† Grace is variously described as "Inspiratio bonae voluntatis, inspiratio dilectionis, caritatem diffundens," all the forms being explained by the change of our substance "in melius," "De Trin.," 5. 16. 17; viii. 923. Also it is the communication of the Divine "esse." "De Spir. et Lit.," 3. 5; x. 203.

infusion of grace means the communication of this Divine substance, and it is so directly of God's will and working, and has so little relation to the historical Christ that He is simply the greatest example of predestination.* Salvation, it is true, does consist in the pardon of sin as well as in the inspiring of justice,† and Augustine's conception of pardon is deeply influenced by Scripture, and it continued to cherish in the Church a more personal sense of pardon and grace. But his own chief interest is in the second idea, and it is steeped in Neoplatonism. The inspiring of justice is the impress of God on the soul, so that, being influenced by the fire of His love, it may abandon the form of worldly (*saecularis*) desire, be formed anew to Him, as it were receiving the impress of immutable form, and so, what it receives from His beauty shall be pleasing to Him.‡ Here manifestly love is not a personal response to a personal appeal of God's love, but is an idea possible for any kind of ascetic pantheism.

This failure to give a due place to moral

* "De Don. Per.," 24. 64 ; x. 1033.

† "Serm.," 251. 8. 7 ; v. 1171.

‡ "De Civ.," 10. 6 ; vii. 283.

personality prepared the way for the later view of the sacraments and for the subjection of the laity. The moment men fail to see that there cannot be any right salvation save into the liberty of the children of God, and that nothing can work that deliverance save what awakens a response in our hearts and teaches us that all life is of God's love, they begin to expect salvation as an external gift. If salvation is an impersonal influx of the Divine, the Church may be its sole sphere, the priesthood its sole instrument, the sacrament its sole vehicle. And, as it is an *opus operatum* in any case, the sacrament may well be of the same nature. The religious life then consists in the one task of making room for this influx and making diligent use of its channels, and so it becomes an affair of asceticisms and observances. For that life moral independence is not a necessity, as it would be if we realised that salvation is a work in our hearts which has its first evidence in transforming the common life into a perpetual working of God for our highest good, our final salvation.*

* An illustration may be found where it is least expected. Charles Hodge ("Systematic Theology," ii. 683)

Augustine's Neoplatonism also helped to fashion his conception of the life beyond the grave to which the significance of salvation had been transferred. The bliss of heaven will be solely the vision of God, and in spite of some Scriptural language, the essence of it is not unlike the Neoplatonic ecstatic sense of being one with God.* Consequently religion was naturally interested in the rites which helped to create that state. And this state, purely as it is attained through God's

says efficacious grace is not of the nature of moral suasion, but acts immediately so that nothing intervenes between the volition of the Spirit and the regeneration of the soul. Truth may accompany, as putting on clay the opening of the eyes of the blind, but "it has no co-operation in the production of the effect," which is not inadequately described by the Schoolmen as "a physical influence of the Spirit." Why then in the name of common sense have anything so indefinite as truth, and not have a vivid sign like a sacrament which, being physical, might be the channel of at least this physical effect? Moreover, the whole view rests on the same idea of omnipotence as plays so large a part in Catholicism. Where it comes in there can be no place for human limitations, or indeed for human life at all under the only conditions in which we know it. All this only proves how much of the old leaven remained in orthodox Protestantism, especially of the Calvinistic type. The result also was other-worldly and ascetic.

* "De Civ.," 22. 29. 6, and 30. 1 ; vii. 801.

justice, which by the gift of God makes us just, is, nevertheless, precisely because it comes from without, still capable of being conceived as somewhat arbitrarily attached to the idea of merit. These same good works of ours, when we understand them to be rather God's than ours, are now imputed to us for obtaining that Sabbath rest.* God reckons His grace our merit.† The Augustinian conception of grace as all of God only needed to be modified somewhat, and the moralistic and transferable idea of merit which plays so large a part in the Roman system at once followed.

But mightier by far than his conception of heaven was the sanction Augustine gave to the popular Catholic conception of hell, in which also his Neoplatonism played a part. To be immersed in material suffering, in hostile matter like fire, is more in accord with his idea of being far from God than any kind of spiritual anguish would have been, so that he even maintains that the devils are subject to physical burning. Primarily, that view belonged to the popular Catholic tradition fed from far distant pagan springs; but the justification of it is his own, and it has nothing

* "De Civ.," 30. 4; vii. 804. † "Ep.," 194. 5. 19; ii. 880.

to do with the God and Father of our Lord Jesus Christ, in whose heaven the angels rejoice over the one sinner who repents, and whose revelation is the shepherd leaving the ninety and nine sheep in the wilderness to seek the one that was lost. It concerns the *summa essentia* which abides in the greater reality the less it communicates itself, which may communicate itself wholly as it will, and which, if it only communicates itself sufficiently to keep a spirit alive in eternal torture, is yet a good in so far as it communicates itself at all.* Thus, by denying significance to the moral personality, he defends an idea which could never be related at all to the Christian idea of God except on the ground that in His eyes personality is so sacred that even He might not rend from it an evil it had chosen. But when condemnation did not regard the moral personality, the way of escape might also disregard it, and be wholly external and arbitrary.

The practical issue among the barbarian peoples was the certainty of everlasting misery "unless one keep the faith not of three Incomprehensibles but of one Incomprehensible." Terrorised by that idea, men became submissive subjects of a Church which ruled like an ancient

* "De Civ.," 19. 13. 2; vii. 641, and 22. 24. 1; vii. 788.

keep by the awful dungeons underneath the foundations. To forget how men believed that, even with Church and sacrament and absolution, they might still come to everlasting burnings, but, without them, there was no escape, is to ignore a chief source of her corruption as well as of her power.

The important matter for the future development was the distinction between the *communio externa* and the *communio sanctorum.* The point had been reached where, through the very success of the Church, such a distinction had to be made, and the future necessarily depended on how the one was related to the other.* As in Israel, so in the Church, it became necessary to distinguish a holy remnant. That it is a remnant according to election agrees with the prophetic conception, and also that it constitutes the true Israel. In some respects

* Sohm regards the identification of the two from the beginning as a chief cause of the development of Catholicism. But so long as the Church was a persecuted minority, it had its fan in its hand, and had a real basis for its belief. Catholicism, in the Roman sense at least, only arrived when, the distinction becoming necessary, the communion of saints was made the essence of the organised society in such a way that what was true of the part was made true of the whole, or rather of the organisation and officials of the whole.

Augustine regards it also as the saviour of the whole society through suffering and service. If it bore fruit in the mediæval papacy it also bore fruit in the mediæval saints and missionaries. Moreover, it nourished a simpler piety, and after many years broke up the power of the very sacerdotal institution it had created, which it was bound to do as soon as the idea of moral personality came again to power. Nor must it be forgotten that the hierarchical and sacerdotal effect was not due to Augustine directly. His own teaching in itself might as readily have developed earlier, as it did later, in a prophetic and not a priestly direction. The fruit it bore was due mainly to the ground it fell on, to the chaotic state of the Empire after the incursion of the barbarian tribes, when men had once more to be taught like children. These two influences, Augustine's teaching and the dissolution of the ancient civilisation through the barbarians, mainly created the Roman idea of the Church.*

* A remarkable parallel is presented by Jeremiah. No one did more to make the prophetic ideas an abiding power in Israel and to nourish the spirit which finally turned away from the priesthood and the temple and the whole priestly ritual, yet the immediate result, as this teaching fell on the political chaos of Israel, must have

He is himself so much involved in this chaos and so impressed by the Church's enormous task in the midst of it, that he is ever apt to transfer the attributes of the eternal society of the elect, which in his reflective thought is alone the true city of God, to the whole actual organised society of the Catholic Church. In the intellectual chaos of the time, it was then easy to tone down or even omit the most characteristic elements in his view of salvation as all of God's grace, and to transform it into a crude idea of salvation by merit, which led to still cruder ideas of salvation by sacraments, saints, and absolutions;* a result which was the easier, as we

been something like the transference of the conception of the holy remnant to the whole of Israel as a religious unit. The result was Deuteronomy and the whole sacerdotal development. The question in both cases is whether the hard shell which the kernel itself will burst is not at a certain stage a necessary protection. Would prophecy have weathered the Exile and a spiritual Christian faith the dissolution of the Empire in any other form?

* A valuable discussion of this point will be found in Bishop Robertson's "Regnum Dei," 1901. Augustine's lofty appreciation of the Catholic Church, he says, "is in no small part the transference to the *externa communio* of the eternal and indestructible prerogatives of the saints in the sense of the predestined, the only real Church in

have seen, because of the absence of any right idea of the moral personality in Augustine himself.

But the opposite element in his teaching, so mechanically combined, tended ever more and more to separate and work apart and finally to come into conflict. Thus it nourished various types of simpler and more mystic forms of piety, and finally became one of the chief causes of the Reformation, and one of the chief influences in the whole thought of the Reformers. And just as we judge prophecy not mainly by its influence in creating the priestly code, but in keeping alive a deeper religion in the hearts of the people and finally in breaking the sacerdotal shell it had helped to create, so we should judge Augustine.

the Augustinian sense of Reality," p. 203. This identification was afterwards accepted with such changes in Augustine's teaching as gave it a new meaning, "foreign alike to Augustinian and pre-Augustinian thought," p. 204. Further, he sees in this the germ not only of the Mediæval but of the Counter-reformation theory of the Church as a *societas perfecta*, p. 214.

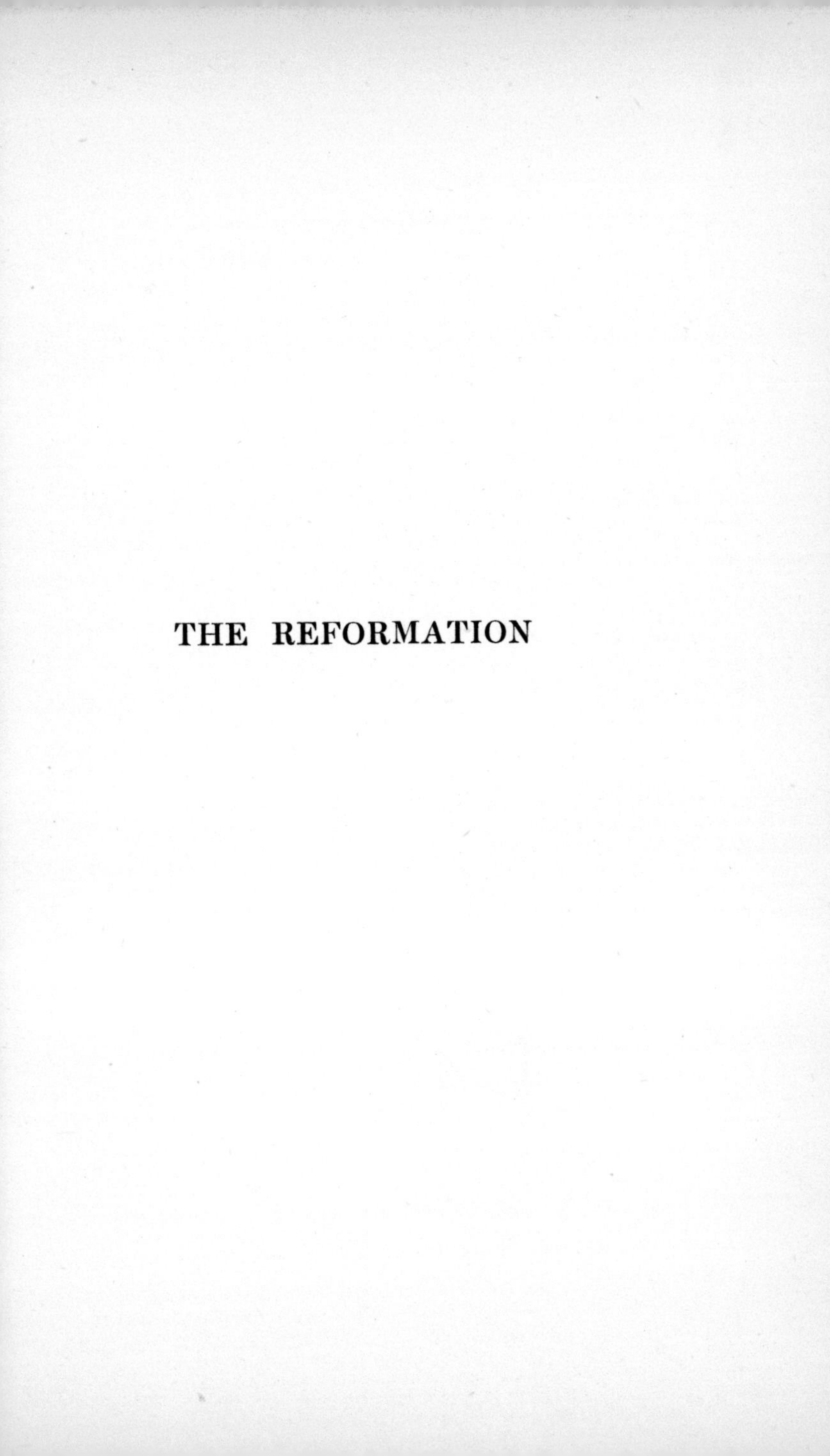

THE REFORMATION

CHAPTER VIII

THE REFORMATION

FROM the beginning it has been recognised that the fundamental distinction between Catholicism and Protestantism is to be sought in different conceptions of the Church. Protestantism distinguishes between the religious idea of the Church and any institution in which it may at any time be more or less adequately embodied, and believes in a unity through faith in the one Head, which is a reality though it be represented by no earthly head or incorporate in no visible institution.

This distinction the Roman controversialist usually treats as a perverse afterthought, a feeble substitute for the actual visible corporation governed by one head, after Protestantism had broken away from it. Even were that a true view, it would not prove the distinction either invalid or unimportant. The

Jew only began to realise what was meant by a spiritual head after the hope of a politically united Israel had vanished. Similarly the divine significance of the discipline of division may be to teach us to take a more religious and less external view of the Church.

As a matter of historical fact, however, the distinction was not an effect but a prime cause of the Reformation. The same influence which consolidated the Roman conception of the Church in the sixth century assailed it again in the sixteenth. In both cases it was the relation of the Germanic races to Rome. But for the nonage of these nationalities, the idea of the Church could never have been so identified with the idea of the clergy. Partly by the very discipline of the Church the Germanic races arrived at moral independence and national consciousness, and so outgrew the kind of authority by which they had been trained. With the growth of the sense of individual responsibility, a development of national individuality kept pace. Thence grew the conviction that no corporation could represent the whole of Christianity, with the result that before ever Protestantism came into existence, its problem was already set. It was the problem of finding room in religion for the autonomy of the individual and the autonomy of the State; and from the days of Wyclif onwards it was seen that no progress could be made in that task till a distinction was drawn between the religious fellowship and the religious institution.

So far no one can say that either problem has been solved, much less that both problems have found a common and mutual solution. But, as these tasks go, the time has yet been short. Neither the Greek nor the Roman Church passed the time of their ferment in three hundred years, and their problems were much more simple.

The problem naturally arose first in England, where a more settled civilisation and greater facility of intercourse than elsewhere had created in the minds of the whole people both a desire for greater freedom and a strong national feeling. At the same time that the individual reached religious convictions which made many things in the Church seem idolatry, and religious needs the organised Church could not satisfy, the national aspirations and the Roman claims came into violent conflict. To that sense of the religious individual and of the national life Wyclif gave expression in his "Treatise on the Church." He went back to Augustine's distinction between the *Corpus Christi verum et simulatum*,* and defined the true body of Christ as the *congregatio omnium praedestinatorum*, the assembly of all the elect.† That, he said, is the Catholic Church of the creed which is the object of faith. Its sole head is Christ; its sole bond of fellowship love; its sole service following Christ in the common life; the sole security of belonging to it perseverance to the end.

Many elements in the new movement were never better stated than by Wyclif. By love all individually elect persons become one person, which is the Church, the spouse of Christ.‡ His favourite interpretation of election is through this idea of the bride of Christ. To be elect is to be chosen to be in accordance with the mind of the bridegroom. That, for the individual and the Church alike, does not mean religious observance, but right living of the common life.

* "Johannis Wyclif: Tractatus de Ecclesia," by J. Loserth, 1881, p. 71. "Vere et pretense."

† P. 2, where he also calls it "Corpus Christi misticum."

‡ P. 20.

Hence there is no such distinction in the Church as priest and people. Even the Pope is but the pastor of a local community and valuable for that only as he is a true shepherd of the flock.* That a visible head is a necessity of the Church's existence is a worldly idea, and, moreover, is a practical denial that there is efficacy in the guidance of her invisible Head.†

The reforms which Wyclif demanded he did not expect from the Pope or even from the clergy, but from the working of the Spirit of Christ in the invisible fellowship, showing itself (1) in the individual devotion of the Christian people and (2) in the action of the civil ruler. In other words, his appeal was to the adult conscience and the civil consciousness.‡ It was still Augustine's thought, but transformed by the rise under new conditions of a new sense of moral personality.

Like many of the reformers after him, he still held to the mediæval view that the power of the State is to be used for the succour of the Church. Yet his appeals to the adult conscience

* P. 19. † P. 5 and many other passages.

‡ For a discussion of Wyclif's whole doctrine of the Church see Lechler's "John Wyclif," Eng. tr., 1878, ii. p. 97 ff., and especially p. 150 ff.

and to the civil consciousness are not two distinct appeals which may readily be in conflict. He makes the old appeal to the State, but not on the old papal ground that earthly power should directly serve the religious organisation. His conception both of the ruler and of the State is so altered that he can appeal to the individual conscience in both. The ruler is responsible for helping forward the reformation of the Church, not as head of the State, but as an influential member of the Church, while the evangelical State itself is the practical expression of love, and not merely of power. The civil consciousness is thus to be the expression of the adult conscience, and to derive power from its approval.

This appeal to the autonomy of conscience and of the State arose from no mere human perversity of certain individuals. In a sense it is the appearance of individualism; in a sense also it is the secularising of Christianity. But all true revival of religion consists in so driving men back on their own souls that they there may find God and their fellow-men, and of taking religion out of the mere ordinances of religion into the common life. The Jerusalem which is to descend from God out of heaven has no temple therein, but the streets of it are of pure gold.

This religious interest in the common life soon made itself felt in the writers and still more in the painters. A Holy Family is occupied in common household affairs; the religious ideal is not a nun prostrate before an altar, but a mother nursing her sick child. Into that world Luther entered, and for one short season was the prophet of the movement. The writings which concern us belong to the year 1520, that brief moment when he stood for his gospel in his own person against the world, ere he had become involved in the practical task of incarnating it again in new institutions and shaping it to the needs of an unspiritual people. Those are the moments of immense importance for mankind, not because we can or ought always to live in them, but because they are the moments of dawn when we see our way ere the dust has again risen upon it, marking our progress but obscuring our goal.

Though Wyclif's "Tractatus de Ecclesia" seemed to have been forgotten, it continued to live in Hus's book on the Church, which is mainly a reproduction, and in many parts even a verbal reproduction, of Wyclif.* Through Hus it reached Luther. The first effect was to enable him to go back to Augustine—that is, behind the discipline which had been created for the barbarian—and, then, behind that, to Paul—that is, behind the whole discipline of the new law to which Christianity had been subjected as it first began to absorb paganism. Luther, thus instructed, had already attained a clear doctrine of the Church ere he came into conflict with Rome, and he forcibly expresses it in the writings of the year 1520,† when the conflict reached its crisis.

That the struggle had begun with the sale of indulgences was no mere accident. That traffic marked both the success and the failure of the Roman legal order. Men had been taught that God must be honoured and conscience satisfied. But it ended in a detailed demand for merit to satisfy a punctilious God, which, precisely because of the awaking of conscience to more than legal demands, drove men to this amazing legal

* "Johannis Wyclif: Tractatus de Ecclesia," by J. Loserth, p. xxvi.

† Most of them are translated in "Luther's Primary Works," by Wace and Bucheim.

method of seeking peace. To Luther it was Judaism, and to Calvin Paganism. Here salvation as merit and God as chief of the State found their expression in a forgiveness which was pure legal condonation by the properly certified State officials. The nakedness with which the traffic went on showed at once the spiritual need which had been created and the utter failure of the old legal forms to give it spiritual satisfaction.

Luther's power lay in the simple directness with which he denied the whole conception of God and of salvation upon which the craving for such things rested. To be saved, he said, is not to avoid the punishments of an angry judge, but to find the forgiving love of our Father. With that forgiveness in our heart, we might even receive the punishment of our sin as a blessing. That is the substance of the Ninety-five Theses and also of the tract "On the Liberty of the Christian."

This tract, "On the Liberty of the Christian," is the greatest of the writings of 1520, just because it goes to the religious heart of the dispute. A Christian, it says, is at once the most free lord of all, and subject to no one, and the most dutiful servant of all and subject to every one. Not by detailed obedience and anxious merit, but by a relation of faith to God, whereby all obedience is at once His work and our willing service, is this freedom alone possible. This freedom, otherwise expressed, is a royal priesthood. The Christian is a king over all things, because they cannot hurt him, but must, through God perfecting His strength in our weakness, turn to the profit of our salvation. Christians are also priests with power to appear before God for others and to teach one another mutually the things that are of God. In that kingship and priesthood, their hearts being sweetened by the love of God, they naturally produce good works. Moreover, they can thereby produce them as the works simply of good men and with a single regard to the advantages and necessities of others, and not as works of merit with a view to being justified. To this true inward life of faith all outward religion is merely scaffolding, necessary but temporal, a thing by which it must live, but by which it may also be destroyed.

God to Luther is the Father of our Lord Jesus Christ, who can in no way be so dishonoured as by doubt of His infinite pardoning love, and salvation is deliverance from self-regarding fear into humble, patient, self-forgetting love of others by spiritual victory over life's ills and direct access to God.

That is Luther's gospel. By it his whole view of the Church is governed, and it is vain to discuss his view of the Church without first accepting or rejecting his gospel. It is a gospel to the individual conscience, and of our relation to others through it and not through human regulations; that is to say, it is primarily a relation to others through the mind of God.

At the same time that the sale of indulgences awoke the individual conscience to the need of seeking an entirely new way of peace, it awoke the national consciousness to the absurdity of being spoiled in so material a cause by alien and probably contemptuous hands. Consequently the next pamphlet is an "Address to the German Nobility." In it Luther explains what significance this Christian freedom has for the common life in the world and in the nation.

All Christians are truly of the spiritual estate, every man in his own office being a consecrated priest. The official priest is not a substitute for this universal priesthood, but an organ of it. The sole necessary common organ is the minister of the word of God and of the sacraments. His distinctive character depends solely on his appointment thus to serve the community, and ends when it ends. His office impresses on him no special character, and in no way raises him above correction by the civil magistrate, who also is a priest. Just as the shoemaker in the exercise of his priesthood must shoe the pope, the magistrate in the exercise of his priesthood must correct him. Wherefore, Luther calls upon the princes to become bishops in time of need and to protect the sheep committed to their care from the wolves in sheep's clothing who profess to be shepherds and rulers. Yet he would not have them use compulsion, as if heretics could be overcome by fire, but rather remove compulsion and set men free to live their true lives. He would have less law of every kind, civil as well as canon. Thereby he would arrive at the substance of the Holy Roman Empire, with the shadow of which the pope has so long deluded the German peoples.

The "Writing on the Papacy," which was issued at the same time, maintains that the true Church and true Christianity are the same. The true Church is an assembly of all on earth who believe in Christ. It is a communion of saints through the Spirit, and is an object of faith, not sight, even as the Spirit is. Its unity, therefore, is spiritual, not material, so that, though believers should be apart a thousand miles in body, in the Spirit they are one assembly, since each preaches, believes, hopes, loves, and lives like the other. This unity is enough to make a Christianity, and no other can. To make Christian unity and fellowship external is pure Judaism. Not according to his body, but his soul, is a man a member of Christianity.

Christianity, then, is a spiritual body, and has only a spiritual Head, Jesus Christ. It has no more need of a corporeal head as pope or bishop, than a living animal has need of a painted head. It is a Divine Order for which the pope cannot be a necessity. "For what necessarily must be, must be needed to make a true Christian; and, if it cannot make a true Christian, it cannot be necessary."

The true Church, therefore, cannot be Rome

or any visible community, for the true Church is holy and believing, which no one can see. Nevertheless, the Church is not without external marks whereby faith can discern it. Where the word of God is present in baptism, sacrament, and gospel, we must not doubt God's power to use them. There, then, we cannot doubt, saints must be, were it only infants in the cradle. Unlike Rome and papal power, baptism and the gospel necessarily must be to make true Christians.

Finally, in the treatise "On the Babylonish Captivity of the Church," Luther distinguishes these necessary marks of the true Church from human accretions. They are subject only to one test—that they make believers, that is, members of the true Church. These marks are mass, baptism, and gospel, and they have all the same content—being all alike promises of God's pardon and grace upon which faith can rest.

That is the test and not an appeal to "what the Church has ordered," which is only an appeal to what the tyrants of the Church, without the consent of the Church, that is, of the people of God, have ordered. It is they who have confused the mass by Aristotelian subtleties about substance and accident, made it into a good work and a sacrifice and a subject of traffic and huckstering. All we need is the simple faith of the common people that the body and blood of Christ are truly contained in the elements, and that thereby we have a divine promise upon which to rest our faith, and which nothing but faith can appropriate. Baptism has suffered similar corruption, having been treated as if it were not penitence and not the abiding divine promise of pardon, but something which required a second plank of safety to be provided in a load of vows, pilgrimages, indulgences, systems. The sacraments were instituted for the very purpose of nourishing faith, and it is the very sin against the Holy Ghost to doubt God's promise of pardon and grace, yet men are told that they ought not to be sure of the remission of sins or of the grace of the sacraments, but to suffer themselves to be senselessly persecuted with contritions, anxious confessions, circumstances, satisfactions, works, and an infinity of such trifles. "I cry aloud on behalf of liberty of conscience."

Every believer has the power to absolve sins

if he can give the assurance of God's pardon and grace. Every believer also has power in word and in sacrament. Yet that which belongs to all no individual can arrogate to himself without the consent of all or the call of a superior. The sacrament of orders, if it is anything, is merely a rite recognising this appointment to minister in the Church. "Anything can be invented above it men please. For conscience' sake we may submit. But that is enough, and we are not to be compelled to receive it as necessary to salvation, when it is not necessary." The ministry, if done in faith, is a religious work, but not otherwise than the work of a husbandman labouring in his field or of a woman attending to her household is a religious work, if done in faith. The Church does not establish or ordain or make anything. It is established, ordained, and made by the word of God. The Church which discerns this word is not an official order to judge it. Not by those who judge it is it discerned at all, but by those who are compelled by an infallible certainty to say it is true.

The Protestant conception of the Church everywhere was a reflection of this teaching.

The essential distinction between it and the Catholic view is not that to Protestantism the Church is a fellowship and to Catholicism it is an institution. To both it is at once a fellowship and an institution. The question is, What is the Church in principle? To the Catholic its determining principle is in the institution—its priesthood, bishops, councils, Pope; to the Protestant it is in the fellowship, in all that is involved in the two or three met in the name of Christ, in the succession of believers, in the bond of love.

This distinction between what Ritschl calls the dogmatic and the ethical-political idea of the Church was made under various forms of expression by all the reformers. The Lutherans, following the "Confessio Augustana," for the most part speak of the "Church strictly so called," and the "Church generally so called." The Reformed, following Zwingli, usually speak of the "invisible Church" and the "visible Church." Neither expression is specially felicitous. It is not a question of more or less definiteness of speech, but of a different way of looking at the same thing; and the true Church is not invisible in the sense of having no manifestation in the world.

But both expressions are seeking to embody the idea that the Church is in principle not an institution but a fellowship, and that the institution is to be judged by the fellowship of believers through Christ, and not the fellowship by the institution. The Catholic seeks the determining principle of the Church in its official priesthood and all that it involves of tradition and sacerdotal function; the Protestant seeks it in all that is involved in the two or three met in the name of Christ and all their abiding influence may mean.

The Church is not, by the Protestant view, turned into a mere Platonic state. God alone knows who these true believers are, and in that sense the Church is invisible. But in every society where God is working through the means of grace, we can be sure they exist; and it is their presence which gives it religious meaning and religious power. Therefore, it is not invisible in the sense that it is not active in the actual Christian society. The presence of the hypocritical and unbelieving adds nothing to the Church, but also takes nothing from it. Hence it is an Anabaptist error to say that "it is not a true and Christian

Church in which sinners are found."* Just because we say it is only God who can separate the false members from the true, we are not to attempt to make the distinction, but to include all members of the visible Church in "the judgment of charity." Nevertheless, it is the two or three who have true fellowship in the name of Christ who are in principle the Church, and who alone are rightly described as the Catholic, the Universal Church.†

* "Formula of Concord," Art. 12. 7.

† This conception finds expression in all the Protestant creeds, the Reformed not less than the Lutheran—"II. Conf. Helv., 17"; "Conf. Gall." 27; Thirty-nine Articles, xix.; "West. Conf.," xxv. The Thirty-nine Articles speak of the visible Church as "a congregation of faithful men," *i.e.*, of men of faith, true believers. That is not to be understood as if the visible Church consisted, or even were supposed to consist, solely of true Christians, but that their presence and fellowship alone constitute it a true Church. In short, this is what the Church is, in spite of the presence of others. Then follow Luther's marks by which it becomes visible, almost in Luther's words, that "the pure word of God is preached, and the sacraments be duly administered." The "Westminster Confession" speaks of the visible Church as also catholic, out of which there is no ordinary possibility of salvation. The most adequate expression probably is in the "Apology of the Augsburg Confession." After conceding that evil persons and hypocrites may be members of the external society

The marks of this Church are: (1) that it has unity in Jesus Christ as its one true Head; (2) that its one treasure is the gospel; and (3), that its one official is the organ of the priesthood of all believers.

The first mark, unity in the one spiritual Head, was not a mere denial of the doctrine of the papacy, but an intense conviction of the reality and power of the union which can be effected by driving each man back upon God. In all the earliest reformers Wyclif's conception of the Church as the congregation of the elect had a vital religious meaning. Because the Church was a fellowship of God's elect for His purpose, to be, in Wyclif's language, one person, the bride of Christ, it could be kept one in the truth and one in love and one in service. It was a mockery to believe that the

which is usually called the Church, and that we can profit by the sacraments though administered by them, it continues "at ecclesia non est tantum societas externarum ritum, sicut aliae politae, sed principaliter est societas fidei et Spiritus Sanctus in cordibus, quae tamen habet externas notas ut agnosci possit, videlicet puram evangelii doctrinam et administrationem sacramentorum consentaneam evangelio Christi" (iv. 4). This is the Church which alone is the body of Christ, is renewed, sanctified, and governed by His Spirit, is the pillar of the truth and the kingdom of God.

pope was a necessity for the unity of men chosen from the foundation of the world to be one in fulfilling the purpose of God.

The second mark is that this society had no need of anything save the word of pardon and grace to be the means of realising this eternal will of love. Here is the one necessary treasure of the Church. This word of pardon and grace, of God's will of love, is the gospel, and it is the content of sacrament as well as preaching. Where it is working in word and sacrament there we may not doubt God's power so much as to question that true believers exist and, in their fellowship, a true Church. Nor is this gospel made void though the ministry of it fall to the unworthy, because its efficacy is not the working of the minister, but of the Head.

The third mark is that the official is only the organ of the priesthood of all believers, and not a substitute for it. There is no religious distinction between clergy and laity. All believers are priests, having access to God and the power to serve their brethren in prayer and admonition. Yet just because all are priests no man may publicly minister in the Church unless he be duly called. However it be given, by the people or their representatives, this call is the sole title to office. It is not given because one man is more a priest than another, but because there are diversities of gifts. All Christians are equal as brethren, but not equal in gifts, and a call is a recognition of a special gift—experience, learning, piety, or such-like—for the service of the community. It is a recognition of God's endowment and so of God's call. Wherefore, such a minister is a true leader and bishop. Yet it is only through the ministry of the word—that is, only in so far as he is the vehicle of the mind of God. Through that ministry of the word has been committed to him the power of the keys, though the power is not his in any exclusive sense. It does not lie in men except in so far as, like Peter, they believe in God's word. Their task is by the pure word to pardon and retain sin, and so drive false doctrine and all the openly godless out of the Church. By the power of the word of God, and not by official authority, they call men to penitence and give them pardon and grace or they show their obduracy in evil.

According to the measure of his gift, this

power of the keys belongs to every believer. Hence the unique, right, and true preaching office is common to all Christians who can manifest God's word in speech or deed. When two or three are gathered together in Christ's name, all baptized Christians have power to forgive sins. Yet, as everything must be done in order, the community chooses some one to be its minister, officer, pastor, relying on the same love which makes one man put his gifts at the service of the community, to keep another silent and attentive. Thus in love the order appointed by the community is to be accepted. Yet any special power of the keys which the minister may have, is not as representative of the community, but only as he may have special opportunity of opening and shutting by the word of God—that is, of declaring God's mercy and judgment to sinful men. Through Christ even an unworthy person may open and shut, for the absolution is mighty, not according as it is spoken, but according as it is believed.*

* This whole conception is primarily Luther's. "For such an office is no more than a public service, in a way entrusted to one by the whole community, which are all equally priests," "Expos. of 110 Psa.," Erl. ed. Bd., 40. 172.

"Further, the ministry of the New Testament is not bound to places and persons, as the Levitical ministry, but is spread throughout the whole world, and is there where God has given His gifts—apostles, prophets, pastors, doctors; nor does that ministry avail on account of the ministry of any person, but on account of the word handed down from Christ," "Appendix to Schmalkald Art.," Art. 26. But all the reformers hold practically the same conception of office in the Church, in theory at least. Nearly all of them deliberately avoid the words *clerici* and *laici*, and Calvin ("Inst.," iv. 4. 9) says that the use of *clericus* has its origin in error, or at least improper feeling, since the whole Church is by Peter denominated *clerus*, *i.e.*, the inheritance of the Lord (1 Peter v. 3). Nor is the power of the keys otherwise understood, even when to the preaching of the gospel was added Church discipline, as in Quest. 83 of the Heidelberg Catechism. It is the assurance of pardon to all who truly believe, and of God's wrath against all unbelievers and hypocrites (Quest. 84).

LUTHERANISM AND CALVINISM

CHAPTER IX

LUTHERANISM AND CALVINISM

THIS doctrine of the Church had to work upon peoples who were still largely under the old ideas and accustomed to the old restraints. Mediæval ideas of the nation as Christianity with the two swords—the ecclesiastical and the civil—still prevailed, and the outward authority of the Church had so long been the sanction of conscience that without it men were as swimmers who had suddenly discarded their bladders. Some rule by regulation and outward compulsion, some force of an authoritative institution, seemed imperatively necessary.

Protestantism was fundamentally an appeal to the religious individual, and its conception of the Church was a fellowship of individuals through their religion; but when it came to dealing with the actual situation, the Protestant had only in a slightly less degree than the Catholic been prepared to do without the succour of outward compulsion. Both Lutheranism and Calvinism began at least to realise that autonomy is of the essence of conscience, that whatsoever is not of faith is sin, that an act is corrupt by the mere fact that it does not spring from our own sense of what is right. Both also began to realise that autonomy is of the essence of a free state, that unless it can develop a government which is subject to nothing but its own national laws, it is necessarily a weak and debased government. Yet from these very principles of freedom men wrung for a time the justification of compulsion. The Lutheran sought it in the autonomy of the State and made the civil magistrate his trust; the Calvinist sought it in the autonomy of conscience and made Church discipline, which aimed at being a corporate exercise of the individual conscience, his trust. Both alike were the outcome of the same spirit which has done so much to determine all forms of the Church, the spirit which wishes a stronger force than persuasion and a more visible security than faith.

In this difference between Lutheranism and

Calvinism we see something of the same difference as appeared between the Eastern and the Roman type. Partly this was determined by the historical fact that Lutheranism developed in alliance with the State and Calvinism in opposition to it, but partly also there was in Lutheranism an Eastern type of faith and in Calvinism a Roman. That sprang, in the first place at least, from different religious experiences. What distressed Luther in the sale of indulgences was the proof it offered of the enslavement of the soul; what pained Calvin was the idolatrous conception of God. The reason was that Luther had been called to freedom through the joyous sense of pardon and grace, and Calvin, by the same sense of wholly unmerited grace, had felt himself a slave to serve the glory of God. Both experiences are realities of faith, and both reformers realised both realities, but the difference of emphasis meant that Lutheranism was primarily a rejection of the Judaic element in the Roman Church and Calvinism of the Pagan.* To Lutheranism salvation was

* Alex. Schweitzer, "Reform. Dogmatik," 1. 16 ff. Discussed by Gass, "Geschichte der prot. Dog.," 1854, vol. i. p. 85 ff.

the freedom of the Christian. In spite of oppositions, evils, and deaths, and in the confidence that even the worst of them will work for his salvation, he is enabled to live in the sense of victory and peace. Rightly interpreted, that ought to mean boundless courage to fight all compulsions with the sword of the Spirit, but it was possible to interpret it to mean that, so long as a man could maintain this inward freedom, it did not much matter about its outward realisation on the earth. The Church has no treasure but the word of God, and it compulsion cannot aid. But if this is a man's true religious life, and if, in spite of all outward compulsion, he can live it, why should not as much compulsion as can do any good lie in the hands of the State?

On the other hand, the Calvinist, who regarded salvation as a life lived wholly to the glory of God so that death itself could not change its activities, naturally resisted any State compulsion, submission to which could not be itself interpreted as obedience to God's word and to conscience. Yet, as compulsion was still felt to be necessary, conscience and God's word were incorporated in the organised society and their dictates enforced by the outward efficacy of public opinion expressed in Church discipline and excommunication. The Christian has no guide but conscience and the word of God, but for that very reason, it was urged, he must submit to their incarnation in the Church.

What kind of ethical-political form, to use Ritschl's expression, Luther thought his dogmatic conception of the Church as the fellowship of believers ought to have on the earth, is difficult to determine. There are, however, the plainest hints that he did not wholly approve the course things actually took. The worldly lords, he says, will in the devil's name always be teaching and schoolmastering Christ how He should conduct His Church and spiritual rule. Government according to the gospel, he thought, could not be till a genuine community had arisen. Still more striking is his desire that those who would in earnest be Christians and confess with hand and mouth the gospel should inscribe their names, assemble apart for prayer, reading, administering the sacraments, and other Christian works, and not only correct, but, if need be, cast out those who do not live Christianwise. This society he has failed to establish only because this matter has not yet been fully discussed and preached of, and he "has not the people for it" and sees few pressing forward.* The Lutheran writers usually regard this passage either as a mere saying by the way † or as a dim adumbration of some spiritual ideal,‡ and in either case of no abiding significance in Luther's view. The reason of these interpretations is that the passage seems inconsistent with his usual opposition to everything resembling a conventicle. "Gott will kein Sonderling haben." But this society is to exist in the Church and not be inconsistent with the administration of the sacrament to the whole community.

Moreover, the idea appears at the time when his hope that the bishops would put themselves at the head of the movement and save it from becoming a mere affair of the princes had been disappointed. His whole opposition to the Anabaptists shows that he could not have dreamt of a Church content to be a

* "Deutsche Messe," Erl. ed., 22. 230 ff.

† Tschackert, "Die Entstehung der Lut. u. Ref. Kirchenlehre," p. 182.

‡ Sohm, "Kirchenrecht," i. 588.

conventicle, content to purge its own borders and attend to its own edification. But may he not have wished to afford the fellowship of the saints a fuller opportunity of expressing itself and of working in the Church by creating for itself special associations within the Church? Moreover, however impossible to realise by any ecclesiastical action, the problem is to have fellowships resting on purely religious ground which shall not be separate from, but contribute to the Church as an ethical association for the improvement and succour of the world at large.

As his hopes from the religious leaders and the religious people and even the religious princes failed, he had more and more to content himself with an educative State Church which would at least serve the primary Christian end of disseminating the word of God. The external appointment thereof he could leave to the princes, because they had been appointed of God to rule in external matters. This attitude was the easier for him that he thought the end of all drew nigh. A strongly eschatological piety made him, like the early Christians, indifferent to forms and organisations and was one of the reasons why he penetrated in so amazing a way to their spirit.

Yet his patience was not always equal to his courage and consistency. At first he would not have Reformed preachers imposed against the will of the people and would empty the monasteries only by preaching. Even Münzer and the Anabaptists he would allow to go ahead and preach what they can and let the word of God take the field against them. But soon his toleration of the Roman clergy and the monastic abuses came to an end, and he wonders that Münzer is allowed to slink about so long.

Compulsion was asked for, not in the interest of religion but in the interest of public order, but it was the beginning at least of the treatment of inward freedom as if it could be cut off from its outward expression and live. To understand the position it is necessary to bear in mind that the Reformers did not think of Church and State, but of a Christian nation with the two swords. Mediæval ideas so far continued to prevail that, on the one hand, society was still thought to rest on the Christian faith as a definite system of doctrine and, on the other, the State, as the result of a long struggle, had come to direct the Church's appointments to office.

Out of this historical position there arose the doctrines that the magistrate is *praecipuum membrum* of the Church and that he is *custos utriusque tabulae.* By these two doctrines Luther's view of the relation of the civil government to the Church may be understood.

The visible Church is to Luther a saving institution in the sense that by it God's word is manifested. That is its whole task and its whole authority. As its most important member, the magistrate has the duty to make it as fit as possible for this task, and forward it as far as possible in the fulfilment of it. He has no power to teach, but when the Church feels the need of true doctrine and wishes to be freed from a false teaching office, he, as chief member, may put himself at the head of the Christian community and act for it as a kind of bishop in time of need. He, too, is a priest, and may for this purpose act for the priesthood of all the Church's members. Thus he may institute a visitation, help in placing worthy pastors and in providing for their maintenance. It is the highest honour of princes that they should honour God's word and require it to be taught.*

The right of the magistrate to use force, however, does not depend on his being the chief member of the Church, for the Church is only served by the word, which force cannot aid. His right to use force depends on his being the custodian of the two tables of the law in the State. The first table refers to the honour and glory of God, and the point of the argument is here. The civil power is not to be an inquisitor of the conscience. In private, men may believe what they will, and, in their chambers, have as many idols as they will; but if, to the injury of the peace of the community, they contend against a public article of the faith, they are to be punished as public criminals. Heresy is a spiritual thing, and can be hewn with no iron, yet the magis-

* Luther drew the distinction quite clearly between the sphere in which the prince could act and that in which he could not. "Principes nostri non cogunt ad pacem et evangelion, sed cohibent externas abominationes" ("Luthers Briefe."—De Wette, Bd. III. 50), but the suggestion that it was part of his service to God to be to his land what a house-father is to his family naturally led to a very wide construction of matters external (iv. 92).

trate cannot suffer his subjects to be led into disunion and division by contumacious preachers, as that would end in revolt and uproar. Only one kind of preaching can be in one place.

To Luther, however, it always remained clear that the work of the magistrate in the Church could never be more than a help to her task of ruling purely by the word of God, and, as Sohm maintains, it was no inconsistency when in later life he protested against setting up ecclesiastical government by the magistrate.* Jurists in the Church, he said, are not jurists but canonists and blockheads, and, as quoted above, it is in the devil's name, not God's, that the worldly lords rule the Church.

* Sohm hardly admits a single limitation of the age in Luther. The evil was all wrought by the small faith of his successors, beginning with Melanchthon. "As the Church of Christ threatened to sink without legal compulsion, men cried in the fear of little faith for—the police. By the constable and the jail the Church of Christ was to be saved, and, to have them, the civil magistrate was necessary (p. 680). Hence a Church ruled by the court instead of by the Holy Ghost (p. 659). In Julius Köstlin's "Luthers Lehre v. d. Kirche," Luther's limitations are fully declared, but, even so, his superiority to his age is scarcely less amazing. An occasional hasty utterance never makes it doubtful that his abiding faith was in persuasion, not compulsion.

But Luther had no successor in this protest. Even Melanchthon came more and more to regard the Church as a school of religion and morals, and more and more there was a desire to rule in it by making excommunication civil as well as ecclesiastical, and punishment corporal as well as spiritual. All this was no doubt of little faith, yet it might not have succeeded had there not been an active principle working for the dominance of the State in religious matters. Not only had the State, to save its autonomy, become the ruler of the Church in point of fact; the State had been recognised as a religious sphere, because the religious sphere was seen to be nothing less than the whole secular life. This exposed men, driven by stress of events, to the idea that the true consecration of the whole life might be sought by the expression of the national life in its civil rulers. In that way a national Church was an advance upon an ecclesiastical institution under priestly rule.

Yet the power which was set up was just the old episcopal power with the single modification that its punishments required also civil sanction. The consistorium, the instrument of the new power, was just the old episcopal court appointed by the civil power. By the end of the sixteenth century these courts were in full operation throughout Germany, and were being justified in theory as well as relied on in practice.

At first something of Luther's idea still remained. Power was only temporarily entrusted to the prince by the law of the land. But presently the government of the Church is said to belong in principle to the civil ruler as the custodian of the two tables of the law. That which was usurped by the Catholic bishop is now said to have been restored to its rightful owner. Thus the Church is put under the State in principle as well as in practice.

Calvin started with Luther's dogmatic conception of the Church.* But partly from his circumstances as the leader of a popular movement usually in conflict with the rulers, partly from temperament, and partly from his conception of serving the honour of God, it was

* Societas sanctorum omnium quae per totum orbem diffusa, per omnes civitates dispersa, una tamen Christi doctrina et uno Spiritu colligata, unitatem fidei et fraternam concordiam colit atque observat ("Op. Cal. (Corpus Reform.)," 5. 394).

a necessity for him to endeavour to carry out this conception in the actual organisation of the Church. What Luther only dimly dreamt of as part of the Church's activity, Calvin attempted to carry out in all her borders. So long as his endeavours were confined to his congregation of French exiles in Strasburg, which was a quite voluntary association, it was an effective expression of this Christian fellowship.* The most manifest power of his teaching has been displayed in churches existing in spite of the State. Not in Geneva, but in France, had it free course. Yet the experiment in Geneva shows how an organisation, admirable as moral suasion, may be a tyranny backed by the civil ruler and the stake. The striking thing is not the nature of the organisation, but the application of it to the old conception of the nation as Christianity with the two swords.

To the Reformation idea of the true Church, as those who are one "by living together under the same Spirit of God, in one faith, hope, and charity, called not only to the same

* See "Calvinstudien," Bohatec and others, p. 294, 1909, in which Calvin's doctrine of the Church, by Werderman is valuable.

inheritance of eternal life, but to participation in one God and Christ,"* Calvin remained true to the end. By the sense of pardon and grace we should feel ourselves engrafted into it. Separation from it is denial of God and Christ, for it is the pillar of the truth and the bride of Christ.† Even though the whole body of the clergy were false to it, and though it were oppressed by councils, the truth would abide in the Church to rise again. Not by subjection even to councils are we one with it, "but if our wish is, as it ought to be, to agree with the Church, the way to do so is to consider and remember the injunction which the Lord has given both to us and to the Church—to obey Him with one consent." ‡

The only treasure of the Church is the word of God. Calvin still, however, identifies true doctrine, not with Scripture, but with preaching Christ.§ The power of the keys is simply a striking figure for the power of the word to open heaven to those who believe. The power of the Church is solely in the use of the word. The only thunderbolt of the Church is excommunication, which has no physical

* "Institutes," IV. 1. 2. † 1. 10.
‡ 10. 18. § "Op. Cal.," 51. 198, 199; 7. 613.

force, but is purely an application of the word, not as anticipating God's judgment, but to guard against injury to God's honour, hinder the evil effects of bad example, and lead, through shame and reflection, to penitence. No true bishop thinks of usurping the power of the sword.*

More and more, however, Calvin insisted on the significance of the visible Church. The article of the Church in the Apostles' Creed, he says, relates in some measure (*aliquatenus*) to the external Church, as every one of us must maintain brotherly concord with all the children of God, give due authority to the Church, and, in short, conduct ourselves as sheep of the flock.† The visible Church is our mother who must give us birth, nourish us at her breasts, and keep us under her charge all our earthly life.‡ "When the preaching of the gospel is reverently heard and the sacraments are not neglected, there for the time the face of the Church appears without deception or ambiguity, and no man may with impunity spurn her authority or neglect her admonitions or resist her counsels

* "Institutes," IV. 5. 4; 9. 10; 9. 13; 11. 3–5.

† 1. 2–3. ‡ 1. 4.

or make sport of her censures, far less revolt from her or violate her unity."* Thus more and more the visible Church comes into prominence as something to which it is necessary to belong in order to belong to the society of God.

The Reformation is not a breaking with this Church, but a restoration to it of its true form, which is not necessarily exactly the form of the Apostolic Church, but a form of which the Apostolic Church can at least be regarded as the standard.† To break with the Roman Church is not to break with this Church, partly because "from the Roman Church we were cast out," and we are prepared to show that this was for the name of Christ, and partly because, while baptism and real churches remain under the Roman tyranny, the papacy is not the bond of the Church but the corruption of it. The Church is the kingdom of Christ, and reigns only by His word, and "the pretence of succession is vain, if posterity do not retain the truth of Christ." ‡

Christ has appointed for the government of His Church the four offices of pastors, doctors, elders, and deacons.§ These are elected by the

* "Institutes," IV. 1. 10. † 10. 30, 32. ‡ 2. 2, 5.

§ "Op. Cal.," 10. 15 ; "Institutes," IV. 3. 4.

congregation, yet that election does not stand for the sovereignty of the congregation, but for the sovereignty of the Spirit of God. The right of the community is the right of their universal priesthood, the right of God's elect who can discern God's will and by His Spirit interpret His word. It does not rest on a democratic basis but on the relation of believers to Jesus Christ, who through them calls those who are to administer His word, not carry out the wishes of their constituents. Behind the whole conception lies the idea of believers as God's elect called from all eternity to be vessels of His mercy to live for His glory and discern His will by the indwelling of the Holy Spirit.

The teaching ministry announce the word and are authoritative in doctrine, and the elders are associated with them in discipline. They do not keep the Church one as God's substitutes; but, to show His condescension and to teach humility, He does His work by their lips.* Their task is to keep the communion of saints together by the two chains of sound doctrine and brotherly charity.† But it is as servants not as lords over God's heritage, and with an eye not to outward splendour but to the things of

* "Institutes," IV. 3. 1. † 2. 5.

the heart. Calvin praises the bishop who carried the body of the Lord in a wicker basket and His blood in a glass, but suffered no man to be hungry; and Ambrose, who broke up sacred vessels to ransom captives.* All ministers are to be equal and no one is to dream of primacy in the Church. Office is service, not power.† Yet the ministry is an office necessary to holy consent in the faith and right order, and for that reason to be held in honour and listened to with respect.‡

This system has been abundantly criticised, but there are two criticisms of special importance. The first is Ritschl's. The Church that is an object of faith, he argues, is only the fellowship of believers. The Church as an institution is the object of loyalty and service, but does not belong to the things of faith. Calvin so far returns to a Catholic view that he makes the latter also an object of faith.§ This faith, by the judgment of charity, receives

* "Institutes," IV. 4. 8. † 4. 3.

‡ The strongest statement is that the ministry is praecipuus nervus quo fideles in uno corpore cohaereant, "Op. Cal.," 1. 562.

§ "Gesammelte Aufsätze: Uber die Begriffe: Sichtbare u. unsichtbare Kirche," p. 88 ff. References to the visible Church.—"Institutes," IV. 1. 2, 3, 7.

as true members of the Church all who by confession of the faith, exemplary life, and participation in the sacraments confess the same Lord and Christ. But he makes this public judgment of the Church void, by allowing a private judgment that individuals may not be in a state of grace after all. Consequently we are thrown back on the ministry of the word as the legal political mark of the Church. That is to say, we come again to the Catholic position of believing in an institution represented by its officials, the pastors and doctors being the bearers of the common confession and the guardians of the worship over against the community. As applied to Calvin himself the criticism is probably mistaken. His object is not to authorise private judgment regarding the worthiness of our fellow-Christians, but to urge that we shall not suffer such involuntary private judgment to hinder us from treating any member of the Church as a brother.* Nor does he make the Church an object of faith in the sense that he makes any particular form of it necessary to salvation.† Of much, however, that has called itself by Calvin's name, the criticism is more just.

* "Institutes," IV. 1. 9. † 10. 32.

Sohm's criticism,* though somewhat to the same effect, has different reasons. The distinguishing mark of the Christian Church is, in Sohm's view, association without legal bond. Rights in the legal sense and the Christian fellowship are contradictory terms. The Church has no power except the word of God, that is to say, it trusts everything to persuasion. But the Reformed Church is in its constitution external, that is legal, rule. The elders exercise discipline. That shows that discipline was not part of the cure of souls, a manifestation of God's word to warn the evil; but was an independent juridical power in the Church for the maintenance of the institution, as worldly institutions are maintained, by punishment. Moreover, this consistory of elders was simply a managing representative committee. But for all Church rule, as Luther understood it and the Early Church understood it, representatives are impossible. Moreover, if every Church must be organised with pastors, teachers, elders, deacons, every assembly for the word, the two or three gathered in the name of Christ cannot be regarded as the Church; but only organised assemblies can. Then, to word and sacrament

* "Kirchenrecht," p. 653 ff.

must be added as a mark a divinely appointed constitution, which thereupon becomes an object of faith, as in the Roman Church.

But why should not the priesthood of believers find its expression in several persons met in the name of Christ and resolved to be under the guidance of God's Spirit alone, as well as in one person? Surely it is not a matter of the number of persons, but of the spirit in which they act. That and nothing else is the vital question.

That the Church should be no mere creature of the State, should be able to act in the world, expressing its conviction and making plain its requirements, being a living manifestation of a true inward fellowship, was a great advance upon the quiescent Erastianism into which Lutheranism was falling. Not only has this teaching of Calvin been a leaven of quite incalculable influence in the Church, it has been an enormous social force as well, working for constitutional government in the State as well as in the Church. That such government is, as Sohm argues, Pagan and not Christian, is surely inconsistent with the historical fact that no Christian nation, with the possible exception of Russia, has failed to develop a constitution and find some measure of true freedom in it, and no non-Christian nation, with the exception of a few attempts in recent years directly under the influence of Christian example, has even tried such a thing. For its effective working, men emancipated from mere subjection to law and ready to die for freedom to follow their own consciences are necessary.

But this recognition of Calvinism as a vast historical force, keeping alive in Protestantism a sense of the Church as no mere creature of the State and making for such freedom in the State as now admits almost unfettered liberty of thought and action, need not hinder us from recognising the defects in its temper.

First of all, we must remember that it wrought with the old conception of the nation as Christianity with the two swords. Calvin taught that the Church is God's kingdom and different from the civil authority, but even in the days when the authorities were against Protestantism, he held that it was the duty of the magistrate to see that no idolatry, no injury to the divine name should exist. Later, he maintained that, while the authorities are to use their own judgment, that is, to determine whether what the ministers of the word submit to them is truly God's word or not, they are to be guided by the word, strengthen the hands of those who teach it, and not to hinder the free judgment of the Church regarding what is against God's honour. Here the danger of the Church ruling the State and becoming a theocracy is manifest, and the criticism is probably right that the system never is found in its purity except where it is compelled to develop itself in opposition to the power of the State.

This danger was increased by the conception of God's honour which dominated all Calvin's theology. It was in Calvin's own hands a noble and often inspiring idea. But even with him it was not the glory of patient, wise love in the face of Jesus Christ; and with his successors the idea of the deity jealous of his honour, which had so long ruled them under the stern discipline of the Roman Church, reappeared. Then legal righteousness was demanded, and little room left for the outcast and the sinner, and God's word was hardened into an infallible, verbally inspired law, and election was no longer a trust that every movement of faith had behind it the succour of God's everlasting love, but was interpreted purely by omnipotence and omniscience.

Thus the temper Romanism had created again triumphed. Men sought in election a sort of assurance like the pope's absolution, but found, as also with absolution, a fear that did not know but that it might be dropped into the abyss, and all of arbitrary good pleasure. The temptation, therefore, to turn election, from being a religious assurance of God's eternal purpose with one's own soul, into a theological basis for all thought about God and salvation, lay in the desire for a guarantee of doctrine and organisation of the old Roman type, a faith that should be correct in its formulas, and correct in its organisation.

CONFORMITY
AND NONCONFORMITY

CHAPTER X

CONFORMITY AND NONCONFORMITY

IN spite of the part played by Henry's divorce, the Reformation in England sprang from the same causes, and followed in the main the same course as in the rest of Northern Europe. Henry's action would have passed as one of the many vagaries of kings towards which Rome had for many a day been only too compliant, had there been no rising forces of nationality and individual conscience behind.

The interest of conscience in the question is usually discussed as if it were mainly a matter of greater or less corruption of the monasteries. But the morals of the individual clergy formed only a side issue. What had been challenged was the Church's moral jurisdiction. Right and wrong, men said, is not a matter of the verdict of the Church but of conscience. Against its verdict legal casuistry under the canon law is no more sacred than under the civil. The Pope's approval or disapproval is just like other people's approval or disapproval; right, if it can stand in the forum of conscience, and wrong, if it cannot. Upon that point the Reformers all concentrated, whereas, like Luther, they mostly regarded the moral failings of the clergy with pity, because unrighteous bonds had been laid on them and neither intellectual nor spiritual help given them by those who imposed them. The corruption which the Reformers unsparingly denounced was the worldly ambition, greed, luxury, condonation of vice which sheltered itself under the authority of the Church and sought to pass as sacred and inviolable on that account.

So high a cause might well have found a better occasion than Henry's divorce. It would be more flattering to the national vanity to be able to look back to a purely heroic action like Luther's attack on indulgences. None the less the same principle was at stake. Luther was angry because other men received indulgences for another world; Henry because he could not himself obtain an indulgence for this. In moral worth these two positions are worlds apart, yet are they concerned alike with the Church's power to make actions right or wrong; and Henry, in his own way, ended, as Luther did, by saying that, if a matter is right or wrong, it is so by God's judgment and not by the Pope's.

Nor may the power which, but for reasons of policy, was ready to grant Henry's desire, denounce the desire as immoral. The more immoral an action the greater the condemnation of an authority which believes itself God's representative to make it right. Precisely against the idea that, if it were wrong, the Pope could find a way of putting it right, and, if it were right, he could still treat it as a question of policy, men's consciences rose in revolt. An uncorrupted moral judgment must be promptly rendered, and purely on moral reasons. As the Pope continually procrastinated and alleged all reasons except moral, Henry himself was naturally confirmed in the view that he was right in morals and only wronged in policy. In consequence he did the only thing that was right in the whole affair on either side. He resolved that, if his cause were just in itself, he could himself pronounce it just as well as any pope. The mass of the English people concurred, not because they approved of the divorce, but because they agreed that an action was right solely on God's judgment, and that only a man's own conscience in the end has authority either to condemn or to acquit him.

Nothing was then left to be determined save the legal consequences, and these, Henry said, concerned his own country alone.

This rejection of a universal papal law with divine sanction, for a mere national law with no sanction save the national consciousness, is sometimes treated as a departure from a larger ideal for a smaller, whereas it is a stand for a larger, a more universally human ideal. Had it been merely a change from Clement to Henry, the gain would not have been great. But the first effect was to withdraw altogether a large part of human life from the judgment of external law. Henry might call himself the head of the Church if he chose, but no one would long acknowledge his right to rule men's thoughts in God's name. And the second effect was to make the judgment of every man over the rest of life, so far as conscience approved of it, as sacred, as divine, as the Pope's.

Henry's action, therefore, was not different in its results from Luther's, and is not the source of the peculiar religious development of the English race. One difference indeed there was: "King Henry's quarrel with the Pope," as Hunt expresses it, "was the accidental means of the Reformed doctrines finding favour with the dignitaries of the Church." * At the time that only meant what Luther had so ardently desired, that the bishops should become chief pastors in the work of reformation. By the reign of Edward, the bishop was no longer the channel of tradition, grace, and authority, but simply the chief minister of God's word and the chief organ of the priesthood of all believers. His existence was not regarded as essential to Christianity, but only as convenient in the circumstances for the English people. Some had more respect for him, some less, but it was good Protestant doctrine to believe that what was suitable could be determined by the head of the nation acting in his religious capacity, and there was no real difference of opinion on the matter.

At the beginning of Elizabeth's reign, the Church had in it no visible division, except in so far as there were in it adherents of the Roman Catholicism of the reign of Mary. Bishop Jewel's "Apology or Answer in Defence

* "Religious Thought in England," i. 8.

of the Church of England" is by far the most important document of the period. With great clearness, compactness, and force it sets forth a position which no one in the Church would have opposed and few have failed to support, at least among the religious people. Conformist and Nonconformist for the last time lay down together in one fold, a fact which ought to make the "Apology" a kind of sacred writing to the English people.

The idea that it represents a *via media* between Protestantism and Romanism can only be maintained in ignorance of the writings of the Reformers. If it represents a *via media* at all, it is between Lutheranism and Calvinism; and the thing it does suggest is that, had the English Church been allowed to go its own way, it might well have been the uniting link between these two divisions, and Jewel's own confidence that the slight difference between Lutherans and Zwinglians would shortly be agreed, might have been fulfilled.

On all fundamental matters, he says, Protestants are agreed. "Nor as touching God, nor Christ, nor the Holy Ghost, nor upon the means of justification, nor yet everlasting life, do Protestants vary betwixt themselves."

Separation from Rome he defends in precisely the same way as Calvin. "Of a truth unity and concord doth best become religion; yet is not unity the sure and certain mark whereby to know the Church of Christ," else the worshippers of the golden calf and those who cried crucify Christ would have had a Church among them and the divided Christians of Corinth have had none. Unwillingly we have broken with Rome, but, when we had to leave the Pope to come to Christ, there was no choice. "If we could only have believed ignorance, error, superstition, idolatry, men's inventions, and the same commonly disagreeing with holy Scriptures, either pleased God or to be sufficient for the obtaining everlasting salvation, that Scripture could be abrogated or the Word of God void, unless the Bishop of Rome approved, there had been no cause at all why we should have left these men's company."

Unless there is some lawful cause of departing, Lot, Abraham, the Israelites, Christ and Paul could be accused of sects and seditions. The sole test is the Word of God. That means Scripture, but as with Luther it is Scripture as manifesting the gospel, not proof texts about doctrines and organisation. Heresy is not a mere matter of opinion, but of forsaking salvation, renouncing God's grace and departing from the body and Spirit of Christ. The gospel is not a boasting or bragging of knowledge, but a law of life. So the Council of Trent manifests itself as a conspiracy and not a council, because it occupies itself defining doctrines not called in question, "but reclaiming the people from no idolatry, taking away no superstition, diminishing no tyranny and pomp."

In exactly the same way also as Calvin he appeals to the Fathers. He builds in no way on their authority, but he adduces them as proof that the present state of the papacy is a corruption, not a continuance of Christianity. All truth and Catholic doctrine can be proved from Scripture, and the value of the early Fathers to Jewel is precisely that they built on Scripture. Nor is there any special authority in councils. "Why, I beseech you, except a council will and command, shall not truth be truth and God be God?" "God is able, will the councils, nill the councils, to maintain and advance His kingdom."

Nor is there any guarantee in succession of popes or bishops. The idea that the Pope is only Peter's successor, "as though thereby he carried the Holy Ghost in his bosom and cannot err, this is but a matter of nothing and a very trifling tale." "God's grace is promised to a good mind and to one that feareth God, not unto sees and successions."

"From the Primitive Church, from the Apostles and from Christ," however, he claims, "we have not departed." But that also does not mean that he sets up the Primitive Church as a standard, or that there is identity with it in every doctrine and ceremony, but only that we are in agreement with it in desiring the absence of worldly pomp and a Church constituted by faith. That only he makes essential to the essence of a Church. The Church is the communion of truly elect souls manifest wherever God's word works in teaching and sacrament.

The ministry to him, as to Luther, is an organ of the priesthood of all believers for use of the keys, that is, the manifestation of God's pardon or condemnation by teaching men what God's word concerning sin and righteousness really is. "And seeing one manner of word is given to all, and one only key belongeth to all, we say there is but one power of all ministers as concerning opening and shutting, men are only Peter's successors as they are Christ's spiritual ministers." Apparently a bishop is to him simply a chief minister, who, if he have the larger responsibility, should have the deeper humility. "Is it so great a matter to have a vain title and, by changing a garment only, to have the name of a bishop," and he speaks of worldly pomp unbecoming not only a bishop but a Christian man.

Had this teaching been permitted free scope, there can be hardly any reasonable doubt that English Christianity would not be the divided thing we see to-day. But such speculations are vain. Moreover, the need of a discipline of division before the Church could be taught to renounce an infallibility which has not been given her and a unity by violence which is alien to her true nature, is already apparent even in this wise manifesto of united Protestantism.

Like Luther, Jewel's interest is primarily religious, not theological, and like him also, he believes force no real remedy for error, but he shows that he has not yet faced the possibility of division which afterwards drove men to force on the one hand and to polemical theology on the other. Christians were to him God's elect with God's "very sure and infallible rule" in their hands, each of them qualified by possessing

God's Spirit to interpret it, while the ministry was a special organ of their universal priesthood equipped for its application. Was it not natural to suppose that they would continue in charity among themselves, one in the essentials of a universal faith, and that, therefore, the old Catholic conception of the Church as the guardian of the one faith in one organisation had been but little disturbed?

Moreover, Jewel, as well as Luther, had not so entirely risen into the realm of faith but that the elements of an appeal both to force and to polemical theology could be found in him, if this hope of uniformity should begin to be shaken. He too holds that a "Christian prince hath the charge of both tables committed to him by God, to the end he may understand that not temporal matters only, but religious and ecclesiastical causes pertain to his office." Moreover, Anabaptists are monsters whom we defy "even unto the devil" and rival Rome itself in repressing by "lawful and politic punishments." These are Luther's doctrines of the prince as *praecipuum membrum* and *custos utriusque tabulae*, with his view that, while a man's inward thoughts concern God alone, the moment they are expressed they concern the civil order. These doctrines belonged to undivided Protestantism and reappear in both the parties into which it soon divided. Toleration would have seemed to either party mere weakness of conviction, and an immense danger to the State. Yet a great advance had been made in this, that the whole domain of thought was delivered from the rule of law, and the judges did not esteem themselves God's vicegerents to send the offender to perdition. It was a great advance, because it compelled the rulers to defend their actions by the known and not by the unknown, which in the end must mean by conscience of right—and not mere consciousness of authority. But they still had a long discipline to undergo ere they could learn the real limits of their jurisdiction.

The reign of Mary had taught convinced Protestantism to maintain itself as a nonconforming religion, had separated out convinced Catholicism, and had thereby left to themselves a middle class who had conformed to both, who were more interested in a political than in a religious idea of the Church, and whose chief thought was that the convinced Romanist was in alliance with the enemy and the convinced Protestant was dividing the national defence. This political idea had an instrument ready to its hand in the bishop's courts which Mary had revived and Elizabeth did not again suppress. Naturally the question of the relation of the autonomy of conscience to the autonomy of the State was definitely raised thereby as it had never been before. To his great loss as a religious force the bishop was on the political not the religious side of the question. Moreover, as if his own court did not show legal compulsion enough, he was involved in ecclesiastical commissions which really replaced his spiritual supervision, not in one extreme case, as with Luther and Henry, but perpetually—courts in which the lawyers exercised the power and the bishops bore the ignominy of representing it.

"It was," said Mr. Frere, "the salvation of the English Church that the decision rested in no more than two pairs of hands." * The first was Elizabeth's, who, he explains, had no manner of religious interest,† and the second Cecil's, who never failed to subordinate any he had to prudence. The saving forces were Elizabeth's statecraft and Cecil's moderation. That estimate, strange to say, is not

* "A History of the English Church," vol. v. p. 51.

† P. 285.

meant to be cynical, and so far as the present legal constitution and worship are concerned, it may be true. But if the salvation of a Church is not in legal forms, if it is in religious power, Elizabeth's statecraft and Cecil's worldly prudence were rather its downfall.

At the opening of the first Parliament, Cecil emphasised in Elizabeth's name the need of "a uniform order of religion." Bills for uniformity repeatedly occupied Parliament, but Parliament was itself too divided in opinion to be entrusted with the task, and more and more the ecclesiastical courts were strengthened and secured from popular influence, till they became the mere instrument for the Queen's supremacy. The Queen, not being much impressed by the apostles' ideas about not wearing jewels or braiding the hair, more and more made the prime concern of the bishop the enforcement of ecclesiastical millinery. No doubt such things are *adiaphora*, non-essentials. But the question now raised was whether the non-essential is the sphere of liberty or of authority. The Puritan who wore his hair long because Laud ordered the clergy to wear it short, was maintaining the important principle that non-essentials are non-essentials.

Nothing could be more calamitous for a spiritual authority than to be mainly occupied in making them essentials. The result was to force the bishops away from the position of being chief pastors and back upon Romish claims. The Church of Rome could insist on every detail, because the smallest detail involved the divine authority of the pope over the individual, and thereby became an essential. But a religious authority which enforced uniformity merely by a standard the Government had legalised and thought it policy to maintain, first rallied against it the forces of religion and then of ridicule, and so evoked both Nonconformity and Rationalism. Without being permitted any real right to express the mind of the Church, the bishops were put in the unhappy position of enforcing in the name of the Church what had really been determined by the State. Then they were expected to succeed by persuasion. We find the Queen with feminine injustice urging the bishops to stand on their own feet and not lean so on Parliament and the Crown; as if, after being made tools of Parliament and the Crown, they could do anything else but lean on them. Being made more and more part of the machinery for enforcing uniformity, they were everywhere spoken of as persecutors, and the characters of men in so false a position naturally gave ever less support to their jurisdiction. The bishop, in short, was made a victim as well as an instrument of the autonomy of the State.

Yet no position has ever been defended in statelier speech. The great classic of conformity is Hooker's "Ecclesiastical Polity," and without the study of Hooker no justice can be done to the position. Yet it is also necessary to remind ourselves that splendour of language can clothe bad argument as well as good.

Hooker's doctrine of conformity rests upon a conception of the Church, and that, like every other conception of the Church, must be understood from his doctrine of God and of salvation.

God, to him, is primarily first cause. His working is the observance of a most exact order or law.* He acts by reason, but that is the same as to say that He keeps "a constant order and law." He is a law both to Himself and to all other things. That law He makes known by special

* I. ii. 3.

inspiration to some, and by the general inspiration of reason given to all, but especially to all Christian people. All law thus has its source in God, and is in a sense His government. In that case it might seem to follow that every man must have in him some reflection of the divine order, but instead we are told that the common man has no capacity for government, is naturally heedful only of his own advantage, and must not concern himself with the policy either of Church or State, but conform to the laws laid down for him by his superiors. On that ground of man's corrupt nature law can only be enforced by human rewards and punishments. "Laws politic are never framed aright unless, presuming the will of man to be inwardly obstinate, rebellious, and averse from all obedience to the sacred law of his nature . . . to be in regard to his depraved mind little better than a wild beast, they force his outward actions to be no hindrance to the common good."* The conception of law thus degenerates into mere legal rule, and we never come within sight of the idea that the last word in the universe may not be the law of the constable

* I. x. 1 and 2.

at all but the law of love, and that to find God may be to be set free from the idea of external law altogether.

Hooker's doctrine of salvation is in accord with his doctrine of God. Nothing is more immediate to our salvation than our persuasion concerning the law of Christ towards His Church. This springs from the mystical union which, in some way not explained, is the sanction of all laws belonging unto men howsoever.* Yet he avoids the usual mystical conclusion that God's law should, therefore, be sought in a man's own soul and its sanction in his own conscience, so that God's law is one with the law of freedom. Instead, he diverges into a discussion of the law of angels, and by contemplating them as the unquestioning subjects of God, finds a sanction for submitting to the authorities. The natural way of salvation is exact observance of God's law. As man has failed in that, God reveals a way mystical and supernatural, a way of faith and hope and love. But that is only another law which God has supernaturally revealed "to rectify nature's obliquity withal." Luther's conception of grace as an emancipating rela-

* I. xvi. 3.

tion to God as Father, making all works good by enabling them to spring from love to God and man, is lost to Hooker and to his opponents alike. Pardon is back on the old Roman ground of legal condonation, which naturally requires as much legal obedience as can be rendered before it acts. This divine legislation is given supernaturally in Scripture. Indeed, the sole business of Scripture is to proclaim this saving legislation, with its laws natural and supernatural.*

The Church, in accordance with these ideas, is a supernatural society concerned with this saving legislation. For this view of its nature two quite different reasons are offered. First, it is a supernatural society because in it we are all joined to God, angels, and holy men. Of that reason Hooker makes no further use, as it manifestly does not lead towards his conception of order purely by submission to authority. The second reason is of more utility. The Church is a supernatural society, because, in addition to the law of all society, which is "consent to some certain bond of association," there are laws appointed by God to supply "the defect of those natural ways of

* I. xi. 5 and 6.

salvation." Thus the bond of the Church is both a "law of reason and a law supernatural." *

These two reasons agree with the distinction which he afterwards draws between the mystical and the visible Church. To the mystical Church, which consists of the saints in heaven and earth, the everlasting promises of love, mercy, and blessedness belong. On the other hand, whatsoever we read of duty belongs to the visible Church.† This latter is one, not through oneness or even uniformity of organisation, but through acknowledging one Lord, one faith, one baptism—the only things which pertain to "the very essence of Christianity."

The second conception he in no way attempts to derive from the former. He does not even attempt to relate the two ideas. By understanding the calling of Christ Lord to be an outward confession, faith the acceptance of certain articles of belief, and baptism a rite admitting into the visible society, he is able forthwith to identify the visible Church with the nation. Luther's conception that one Lord, one faith, one baptism are all expressions of

* I. xv. 2. † III. i. 3.

the one gospel of pardon and grace, and that the visible Church is related to the true Church because it has in that gospel the means of a true confession, a true faith, and a true penitence, nowhere appears.

To Hooker, every nation professing Christianity is a Church. The Church and the State are merely two aspects of the same society, which has as much right to determine how men shall worship as how they shall pay taxes.* The authority of the Church, which it is mere insolence in the individual to question, is in the last issue the authority of the Queen.†

* Book VIII. i. 2, though probably not Hooker's own words, expresses precisely the assumption of his whole argument. "Such societies as do embrace the true religion have the name of the Church. The Church of Christ is every such politic society of men as doth in religion hold that truth which is proper to Christianity. . . . The name of a Church importeth only a society of men, first united into some public form of regiment, and secondly distinguished from other societies by the exercise of the Christian religion. . . . There is not any man of the Church of England but the same man is also a member of the Commonwealth; nor any man a member of the Commonwealth which is not also of the Church of England."

† In IV. xiv. 7, the ecclesiastical and civil estates are Aaron and Hur sustaining the only hand which raised up

Whatsoever government a nation, in the capacity of a Church, appoints for itself is right. Though episcopal government is ancient and almost universal, he refuses to oppose Cartwright's divine right of presbyters with a divine right of bishops.* Geneva may govern her Church by presbyters so long as it is merely what is thought convenient for itself, and not "tendered unto the people as things everlastingly by the law of the Lord of lords."† The Scripture has authority in matters of salvation, but the organisation of Churches is left to reason, which, in this case, means the national legislator.

and maintains the state of reformed religion, and in the Dedication of V., paragraph 10, the true inscription of all Churches in the realm is "By the goodness of Almighty God and His servant Elizabeth we are." But everywhere authority to make or refuse change means the State, and that means the Queen, as III. xi. 1. He does mention a Church Council as something the Puritans ask for, but not as a necessary expression of the Church or as something for which the authorities have any need to wait (Preface, VI. 4–5). He there also defends "her sacred majesty's court of High Commission." That, as a matter of fact, is what he is defending throughout. He is not, as his argument often leads us to suppose, a mere assailant of dogmatism, but an unfaltering champion of authority. Forgetfulness of that fact has greatly added to his reputation.

* III. x. 5. † Pref., II. 2.

By proceeding from that source it becomes law, and not merely enforces but enjoins. This quality of law is derived from the nature of all societies. It is not directly a divine right in the Church, but a right depending upon an implicit social contract in the State. Though man knows God's laws by the direct light of nature and reason, the duty of submission to the State is rested upon pure individualism. All men alike are naturally free, but being all alike naturally self-regarding, they have consented to the imposition of laws, and "we being alive in our predecessors have given our consent."* Man is, therefore,

* I. x. 8. The theory of the divine right of bishops which appears in the later books is sometimes ascribed to Hooker himself, but the logical outcome of Hooker's position is Hobbes, not Laud. Yet Butler as certainly as Hobbes founds upon Hooker. The common idea that the judicious Hooker is a consistent thinker who finds the golden mean between all extremes is an illusion. His theory is as dead as Cartwright's doctrine of infallible scripture, and his polemic frequently merely scores off the extremest utterances of the Puritans without touching the heart of their contention. But the interest of his work is, in a sense, its inconsistency, with its germinal hints of the thoughts which were to occupy the English mind for more than a century. The Deists, and particularly Tindal, find their starting-point in the distinction between natural and supernatural revelation, while the whole apologetic of the

in a dilemma, and must choose between conformity to the authority of the State, or exposure to the unrestrained selfishness of wild beasts. As the Church is identical with this society, it requires to be ruled from above in the same way. The Church being identical with the State, its members are no better, and are as much in need of repression. Though too careful in speech to commit himself to Whitgift's language, Hooker continually shows his agreement with it. "The Church now being full of hypocrites, dissemblers, drunkards, and whoremongers, they would choose ministers like themselves, so that what they require is not more liberty, but a stronger hand over them, the troubles of the Church being due not to the rigour of the bishops but to the lack of severity."

There is such a thing as a law of nature and reason, which nature teaches to all who will learn and reason shows to all who will see. The ultimate authority of this conscience of right, he thus admits in theory, but he never acknowledges that it can be put into

next age is not a defence of Christianity, but a defence of the foundations of an institution which could be believed in as men believe in the State.

practice. Not only have the authorities unquestioned control over everything which cannot be challenged with demonstrative reason, but practically he denies that any one is ever in a position so to challenge them.* "'That things doubtful are to be construed in the better part,' is," he says, "a principle not safe to be followed in matters concerning the public state of a commonweal."† There is no such thing in Hooker's eyes as a sphere where law is not in place, or where it may even hesitate. It is the individual who must do all the construing "in the better part." The individual can only proceed on reasons demonstrative, a reason demonstrative being one to which "no man who considers it can withhold his consent."‡ On that principle there will certainly be few innovators upon things as they are, and the safest way of framing our lives is to study willing obedience to man whatever is to be said of God, and there can hardly be any limit to "the utmost of that which is due."§ Even conscience never enables a man to get

* Pref., VI. 5 and 6.

† Pref., VIII. 13. The whole theory of Tudor government is contained in that sentence.

‡ Pref., VI. 6. § III. ix. 3.

beyond "his own only probable collection."* Thus though men should be persuaded that laws are against the law of God, they are bound, for the time, to suspend their persuasion —the time apparently being so long as the authorities are of the opposite opinion.†

The inward meaning of this position is plain. The Protestant trust in the autonomy of conscience having failed to secure uniformity, conformity must be secured by the autonomy of the State. This was a revival of the old Romanist idea that the injunctions of authority turn non-essentials into essentials, with the autocracy of the State in place of the infallibility of the pope, to the end that, as uniformity had not been secured from within, it might be enforced from without.

The upholders of that position could not stop where Hooker did. As they could not follow Hobbes in basing authority upon natural anarchy, they had to proceed to found it upon a divine hierarchy, and to maintain the divine right of kings and bishops. Nothing but such a divine right could turn non-essentials into essentials, and make them

* Pref., VI. 3. † Pref., VI. 6.

the sphere of law, not of liberty. Bancroft and Laud, in making such a claim of divine right, were only justifying the right of the ecclesiastical courts to establish themselves not on, but over, conscience, and their arguments from the Fathers and from Scripture were mere buttresses to a building already erected for ecclesiastical reasons on political foundations.

Hooker's opponents, the Puritans, were also aware that uniformity was passing, and they were as resolute as Hooker to maintain as much of it as they approved. They were willing enough to receive succour from the State, but were met by the obdurate fact that the State was against them. Yet, as little as Hooker, could they entertain Luther's solution of "less law of all kinds." They also, in a different way, fell back on the old Roman temper and made law, in another form, their trust. This law they sought in an infallible Scripture and a theological doctrine of election.

Their conception of the Church also rested on a doctrine of God and of salvation. As with Hooker, God was primarily first cause and absolute governor, and salvation was something which could be given and externally guaranteed. That is to say, their conception of God and of salvation was also primarily legal. They also had moved away from the freedom of the Reformers, from Luther's sense of the joyous trust in God which overcomes the world, and even Calvin's triumphant sense of being an unconquerable instrument for the glory of God. God was interpreted as omnipotence and omniscience, and salvation as something His fiat of power could give or withhold. His word was identified with an infallible Scripture, and His grace with an infallible election. The change is most apparent in the changed significance of election. To the earlier Protestants it was a religious assurance of being chosen by God for victory over the world and for serving His glory on the earth. To the Puritans it was a theological doctrine of salvation by the fiat of the Almighty. The same feeling wrought in it as, in other days and under other conditions, had made men turn to priestly absolution and papal indulgences. Man sought a hard-and-fast legal security, and the same result of uncertainty and terror followed.

But an infallible Scripture and an infallible

election seemed to guarantee the one faith and the one divine organisation which the State might rightly be asked to enforce. Could anything less be attained by persons wholly at God's disposal and with God's infallible law in their hands? With that guarantee the Puritan felt secure in relying on the guidance of the Christian conscience, and he only wished to use the State to emphasise its verdict.

That reliance upon the conscience of the elect person enlightened by God's infallible word gave him a view quite different from Hooker's of the Church as a divine society. Like Hooker, he held the true Church to be the fellowship of saints in heaven and earth, but, unlike Hooker, he was not satisfied to see no connection between that idea and the visible Church, or to identify this latter directly with the baptized nation. Though he never proposed to limit the visible Church till it should be itself a communion of saints, he did conceive that in principle it was that communion. In spite of all hypocrites and evil persons, it ought on the judgment of charity to be treated as that society, and its worship and organisation should proceed on that principle. His estimate of mankind was no more optimistic than Whitgift's, but his outlook was wholly different, because he believed that the elect really could be the salt of the earth. In that case the Church, though still identified with the nation, was no longer in the same way identified with the State. It could be governed by its own spirit from within, and did not need superintendence from above. The people were the Church, and the people, saved by the elect in their midst, were a divine priesthood, of which the minister, whether bishop or presbyter, was but the organ. Having the Spirit they are enabled to discern spiritual gifts. Therefore they ought to choose the minister, whose whole significance lay in representing their priesthood. Excommunication was a right and duty of this society, and should only take place through its representatives, and should only be from its privileges, and not be mixed up with social and political disability. At most the State might be asked to enforce the Church's decision on matters concerning the whole national well-being. There should be no danger of believing that the building and not the society was the Church, none that ceremonies and not the life were the end of worship, none that the minister was more than the vehicle of the message of God.*

Though all this is very unlike Romanism, and though the Puritan had made the enormous advance upon Rome that he based his conception of the Church on the common Christian conscience, an important truth of Romanism was recovered, that the Church must have its own life expressing itself in its own way in the world. With that also it must be recognised there have returned the temptations of Romanism — clerical rule, and inability to see clearly the line between legitimate spiritual influence and political interference, and hence difficulties with the State. Puritanism, holding like Romanism a belief in a religious order higher than the political, was constantly tempted

* From Hooker one would gather that the whole dispute was about bishops and lay elders. Even Cartwright is somewhat caricatured, and the average Puritan was better represented by the Millenary Petition than by Cartwright. There no objection is offered to bishops, and it only asks that ministers be able and sufficient men to preach diligently. All that is said about ceremonies is that the cap and surplice be not urged. The emphasis of the petition is on the abuses of the ecclesiastical courts, with their oppressive delays and their excommunication by lay persons and for "twelve-penny matters."

to forget that it only remains a higher order so long as it does not come down into the lower, that it is a religious order only when it uses religious not political means.

Hooker, therefore, rightly perceived that, however much it might wish to use the State, the instincts of Puritanism were nonconforming. Even in its Presbyterian form and as an established Church it has, compared with the Eastern or the Lutheran or the Anglican Churches, been a nonconforming faith.

This view of the Church as resting on the common Christian conscience had also its effect on the Puritan view of the State. The sphere of the State was no longer everything not demonstrably wrong, but only that which was demonstrably right. The non-essential was the sphere of liberty not of law, because it was the sphere in which every elect soul must be guided of God. In business, for example, the Puritan asked freedom, not on any ground of individual competition, but that he might, as a chosen vessel, live his common life and exercise his stewardship over the goods God had given him, as God required. No doubt the leaven of the past intolerance and reliance upon the secular arm still wrought in him, but there was also the leaven of the new spirit of Christian liberty, with regard to which the only regret is that it has so imperfectly prevailed to this day.*

However much they differed in other respects, the Episcopalians and the Presbyterian Puritans were agreed that the whole baptized nation was the visible Church. But

* No justice can be done to Puritanism unless we remember that it was primarily a religious movement based on religious conviction. Compare, for example, Overall's "Convocation Book," the confession of faith of the High Church party, with the "Westminster Confession" of the Puritans. The former is mainly concerned with matters of government, the latter mainly with religious matters of faith, repentance, and good works. After the view of the duty of the State and the theology based on election and infallible scripture in the "Confession" are omitted, as practically all Churches who now receive it do omit them, its really valuable part remains; whereas in the "Convocation Book," Jesus Himself was a very thorough conformist to the ecclesiastical government, respecting the high-priests and their authority, making no new laws but expounding the old, erecting no particular congregation, omitting no circumstance, ceremony, or duty ("Library of Anglo-Catholic Theology," p. 100, 1844). The Westminster divines, however much they may esteem their Church order scriptural, have a different use for Jesus Christ. Yet the mild "they do greatly err" with which the "Convocation Book" condemns, compared with the anathemas of the Council of Trent, shows that the long conflict had not been in vain for either party.

with the Independents a new type of nonconformity arose. It began with Robert Brown, who wished a Church "of the worthiest, however few," which would proceed with the reformation of the Church "without tarrying for any." Its starting-point was the original Christian view of the Church, as the two or three met in the name of Christ, of which there is no finer account than Hooker gives in rejecting it: "There are which hold that the presence of a Christian multitude and the duties of religion performed among them do make the place of their assembly public; even as the presence of a king and his retinue maketh any man's house a court." *

That assembly alone the Independent held could be the sphere of the ministry of the word, and no authority wider than that sphere could, he thought, be a religious authority. This conception is not properly described as sectarian, as if it could have been satisfied with congregations of true believers while leaving the rest of the world to its fate. On the contrary, it was held that only in this way could the world ever be leavened with true Christianity, that all attempts at a

* V. xii. 2.

wider authority were divisive, and only by this limitation could all Christians ever be united in charity. Their maintenance of infant baptism, their continued belief in election as guaranteeing the Divine order, of Scripture as the Divine law, and their desire at the Restoration to be tolerated as part of the national Church, show how much the Independents were still attached to the idea of a universal Christianity. Their present position is not the result of their theory of the Church, but a departure from it under what has influenced all Churches in the same direction—rationalism and evangelicalism.

RATIONALISM AND EVANGELICALISM

CHAPTER XI

RATIONALISM AND EVANGELICALISM

FROM the commencement of the Reformation another conception of the Church appeared in forms which are not unimportant because they were singular. So far were the Anabaptists from endeavouring to identify the Church with the civil society, that they held it to be a community of saints standing over against society — society being not the Church but the world. Yet they did not accept the modern view of a Church as a voluntary society for the culture of the Christian life. They, too, were burdened with the task of setting up the kingdom of God, and even their vagaries were nourished by this true ambition. They began with the right method—mortification of the flesh and repudiation of all worldly use of force. They desired, at first only by spiritual means, to make an end of all dominion, and not even to seek by law the recovery of goods injuriously taken. Their last thought was to set up by violence a kingdom of the saints.

They built solely upon individual inspiration, without any concern for the historical faith and the historical society, or for the task of turning the civil society as far as might be into the Kingdom of God. The Reformers, being wholly concerned with these tasks, naturally opposed them. Unfortunately it was mainly with the weapon of violence, thus attacking the only thing that was fundamentally true in the position. Even Luther who had advised that Christian persuasion and not State repression should take the field against them, fell from his faith. The result was a barbarous suppression which drove them to the violence they had so earnestly repudiated.

The movement was driven underground, but violence is no answer to the demand to hear, and hear only, the Spirit. Hence it soon reappeared in many strange sects, of which the Quakers alone have retained the first ideas of non-resistance and government by the Spirit.

The extravagances of these sects should

not blind us to the fact that they reasserted important Christian truths. They expected, as Hunt says, like early Christianity, that by making sure of the life or spirit of the Church, the body or form would take care of itself. They also taught that the Church, though in the world, should not be of it, and that nonconformity to society as it now exists is of the very essence of Christianity. Wherefore, though it is true that they rejected responsibility for the imperfect, slow processes of God, and taught a mystical conception of God and of salvation which denies religious meaning to the whole struggle of history, it is also true that they taught much-needed ideas of freedom, of direct religious experience, and of that faith in the immediate presence of God which should enable us to meet evil with other means than violence. After all, progress has mainly been made by people who are so dazzled by a new and intense vision of one side of truth that they have failed to see the other side. The demand of the scholar and of the ecclesiastic that men's systems should form a completed circle is always a barren and a vain demand.

The new wine of freedom, however, which

really burst the old bottles, was intellectual, not religious. Although it had no direct dependence on movements like Quakerism, except in so far as the protest of each sect had helped to create a freer atmosphere in which to grow, Deism was just a secularised version of the doctrine of the Spirit. Individual conscience was the basis of all religious truth, and history was only of value as it reaffirmed the witness each man has of God. And on that basis of the authority of the individual mind the whole modern intellectual world has been built. The idea that authority in the old sense has any place in it rests on a confusion between what is immediate and what is ultimate in knowledge. In all departments the larger part of man's knowledge is held without personal investigation, but the basis of modern knowledge is personal investigation, and the basis of authoritative knowledge is a direct communication regarding which there is to be no question save the authority of him who gives it. The departure from that basis of knowledge has been too fruitful for mankind to return to authority, at least till they revert to barbarism.

Furthermore, this movement has deeply

affected our religious outlook, and more particularly with regard to our views of Scripture, of sin, and of the sphere of religion. That means a great change regarding God and salvation; and though at present it has mainly led to confusion, ultimately it must lead to a great change in our view of the Church.

Scripture has been subjected to the ordinary methods of historical criticism. It matters not what particular results have been reached, it is no longer authoritative in the old sense of "thus saith God and thus shall man unquestioningly receive." It is a book in which God has to do with men, primarily because they have had to do with Him. It tells how, in the struggle of weakness, temptation, aspiration, and of being faithful to the highest they saw, men found that eternal life which judges not by mass and power, fears no more corruption and decay, gives victory over time and chance, sets men free with the liberty of the children of God, so that it speaks to us now not with the authority of a vanished past, but because we also are willing to take up the same struggle and prove for ourselves the same succour of God.

Of the highest revelation, Jesus Christ Himself, this is most of all true. He is supremely the object of religious faith, because He was supremely the subject of religion, because in that dialogue between God and man, in which God reveals Himself, the human part no more perverts the divine. Nor does He ever speak to men except on the ground that they themselves, if they do not wilfully pervert that dialogue, know what He says to be true.

With regard to our view of sin, what may be called an authoritative metaphysic has lost its force in men's minds. Mankind is no more a *massa perditionis* out of which a few are saved into the ark of the Church. Such a view no longer satisfies our idea either of God or of man. The influences which have affected us are partly scientific, partly religious. Slow processes of evolution may accord with a long and patient dealing with man which might so respect man's freedom as to fail, but it never can receive a religious interpretation on the ground of a God

> "Who as it pleases best Thysel'
> Sends ane to heaven and ten to hell";

and just as little does it agree with our

deeper study of our Lord's teaching, as one who came to seek and to save the lost, and who revealed the Father in whose heaven the angels rejoice over the one sinner who repents. And mankind, at various stages of progress with religions struggling painfully after light, and our varied humanity with multitudinous motives, never perfectly good or perfectly bad, cannot be classified as saved or lost on any ground of creed or Church connection, or in that radical way, on any ground whatsoever. The thing that meets us is the old distinction of being saved and being lost; of facing upwards or downwards, with a return to our Lord's teaching that the supreme consideration is not the absence of evil but the presence of good, with His emphasis not on moral attainment but on moral earnestness, not on resoluteness of purpose but on sensitiveness to truth and openness to appeal.

Above all, serious thought in our time has been driven to one idea—that we must seek the spiritual in the sphere of freedom. Material law has annexed the whole realm of things necessary. The old sense of our limitations still remains. "How free we seem, how fettered fast we lie." We can still use the old language and say that all we are is of grace and not of works. Mere fulfilment of our ethical resolves would leave us with a poverty-stricken hope. Yet all God's dealing with us is to set us free, or else it has no other interpretation than the physical nexus of cause and effect, and looks forward to no goal of events, no purpose of the ages.

Manifestly we have here ideas of God and of salvation which, however dimly they may still be looming upon our horizon, cannot be made to accord with any idea of the Church which has held men's minds from the fourth century until now. No more than in times past will we reproduce our Lord's idea without immersing it again in the legal order, but it is equally certain that there never was a time which called so loudly as our own for regenerating our conception by bringing it again to the test of the ideal. Never was there an age which brought men so unavoidably to the issue that the basis of the Church is freedom, not authority, individual faith, not organised constraint, prophetic hope, not priestly tradition. On this basis of freedom two influences have been at work, building up what ideas we at present have of the Church, and still more determining the practical situation. From lack of more precise phraseology, these movements may be described as Rationalistic and Evangelical.

The Rationalistic tendency maintained the old view of the identity of the Church with the civil society. But from Deism onwards it argued that if that is to be possible, the Church must simply be a sanction of the moral commonplaces. The Apologists of the eighteenth century, having the same view of the Church and being forced to defend not Christianity but the universal recognition of it, were slowly driven to accept this issue. Starting with Charles Leslie's conviction that no one but a knave or a fool would question the foundation of the Church as it now stands in all its beliefs and all its outward order, the race of Apologists ends with Paley, who is content to defend Christianity as a miraculous evidence that a purely utilitarian morality has the sanctions of God's command and of everlasting happiness.

In various forms that solution of the problem has continued to this day. Religious association on the basis of freedom seems to be possible only on the ground of the universally accepted. Have we not task enough, if we are concerned, in God's name, to forward the moral well-being of mankind? Why not have one great ethical institution which we are content simply to baptize into the temper and spirit of Jesus Christ?

With Pascal and Butler an apologetic of a different temper appeared which manifestly, if only half-consciously, said Christianity cannot be maintained on the authority of a universal institution or of a universally accepted intellectual argument, but requires for any true acceptance of it spiritual conditions. Perhaps it is not unimportant that both, though belonging to dominant Churches, had been in the position of dissenting from them.

Intellectually Evangelicalism still held an unquestioned position, so that well on in the nineteenth century Leslie could still be published under its auspices. But practically it accepted the position that religion will only appeal on religious grounds. It abandoned the part of the old position which Rationalism had retained—no longer identifying the Church with the nation, but in its heart of hearts restricting the Church to those saved after a very definite type of religious experience. And it retained what Rationalism had abandoned—the infallible word of God and the unquestioned body of Christian doctrine. Moreover, it revived the old Protestant and especially the old Calvinistic ascetic feeling towards life, which more definitely marked off the Church from the world. The practical result was the creation of several new societies, especially the Methodist Churches and the Churches which make up the United Free Church of Scotland, on the recognised basis of free association for the culture of this special spiritual experience of conversion and the propagation of the gospel as interpreted by that experience. Under its influence, moreover, all Churches came to be regarded in the same light of free societies for the culture of the spiritual life and the spread of spiritual influences, the established Churches being different, not because they could be identified with the nation, but only because they enjoyed privilege and aid from the State, or because they lost freedom through its control.

In what we have widely called the Rationalistic movement, a genuine truth of Christianity, that the religious life is just the ordinary life properly lived, has succeeded in such a way as to divert interest from the Church altogether and to teach men to expect to find the ethical society which will work on the whole community in the State, and no longer in so divided an organisation as the Church. With regard to what we have broadly called the Evangelical movement, the effect has been that, with the cooling of the religious fervour, the self-denial, earnestness, and industry which had been taught by the world-denying character of the movement, has proved an enormous power for accomplishing material victories in the earth, creating vast organisations, vast industries, and vast wealth. The result is that the genuine fellowship amid various classes, simplicity of life, and the unworldly spirit which the old Evangelicalism did wonderfully create, is now being sapped by its own success. Congregations of wealthy persons are gathered in one place and of poor in another, and worse still, the rich condescend to the poor in congregational missions, and the prosperous business man seeking to run Churches as prosperous business concerns is established in power in too many congregations. The religious impulse naturally fades more and more, and a dominant respectability turns Christianity into a Phariseeism whose whole moral standard is negative, which has no place for the publican and the harlot, and which occupies itself largely with taking the mote out of its neighbour's eye. That the beam of social and spiritual pride is in its own eye, it overlooks, and the consequence is a loss of any deep passion either for reality or for justice.

Finally, these streams of Rationalism and Evangelicalism could not for ever flow apart. As their waters mingled, men began to see on one hand that a religion of what is universally admitted will always be in the rear of progress; whereas religion, if it is anything, ought to be in the van. Moreover, it becomes plain that religion lives not where everything is undenied and undeniable, but in the vision of things unrealised and by human means unrealisable. It must ever be groping after God and be surest of God where life's stress is greatest and where things must be proved by the venture of faith. On the other hand, Evangelicalism has been taught the poverty of a mere appeal to the religious emotions and the need of a more continuous view of history and of a wider outlook on life.

The old Evangelical impulse is fading, and many are mainly conscious that our emotions are dull, our aims divided, and our spirits dwelling apart. That feeling was mainly responsible for the return of a large section of the Church of England to the idea of the Church as one continuous external organisation. The power of this revival lay in the need of a protest against the conception of the Church as a congeries of rival associations, of competitive religious clubs. It has forced upon us the questions of the idea of the Church, its true unity, its historic task. It has emphasised the Evangelical view that the Church is a religious society not to be identified with the civil society, and has added that it must be a society responsible for a national service, while maintaining that it cannot be identified with the civil society, but should have a life and rule of its own.

The failure of the movement to satisfy those who are convinced that both Rationalism and Evangelicalism have contributed permanent elements to our religious life is not due to the weakness of its historical views about apostolical succession. We sympathise with a man who has any chance of tracing his pedigree from a

Norman conqueror when he helps himself out a little by his imagination, and we should be still more tolerant and sympathetic when there is a chance of showing a pedigree from the apostles. The failure lies much deeper. It is the failure to commend either the idea of God or of salvation which it assumes.

Take, for example, this account of the Church as "a covenanted sphere": "Suppose some wealthy man was desirous of spending money year by year to relieve persons suffering from sickness. He might choose one of two ways of so doing. He might say, 'I will make it known that I am ready to relieve every sufferer who comes to my door,' or he might say, 'I will fix upon some particular institution in which to carry out my resolve: I will select some hospital, and my help shall go to sufferers through the authorities of that hospital.' In the latter case the hospital would be the place where the rich man's promises would be made good; the hospital would be the place where, without doubt, sufferers might partake of his benevolence. In other words, the hospital would be the 'covenanted sphere' of his generosity, and no sensible person would dream of going elsewhere for a share in the rich man's benefactions." *

Manifestly, we must be convinced that this is how the rich man would act, before we can be interested in determining which is the right hospital. If our view of God is not merely that He does not restrict men to His hospital, not even that He succours all who come to His door, but that the supreme revelation of Him is that He seeks and saves the lost and is for ever coming to our door by every device of providence and grace, restrictive ideas of the Church do not touch us, and such a matter as whether orders have been uninterruptedly and correctly transmitted has no religious significance. All conceptions of God are inadequate, but if we feel that our inadequacy lies in our inability to measure God's manifold wisdom, His patient love, His infinite succour and appeal, His joy over one sinner who repents, we are apt to think that the particular road by which His child returns will not matter to Him, and that every Church by which the publican and the harlot enter the kingdom of God will be a true

* Vernon Staley, "Plain Words on the Holy Catholic Church," p. 3, 1891.

Church, and that it may exist wheresoever Christian faith and fellowship exist, wheresoever two or three are gathered in the name of Christ.

Furthermore, our idea of salvation must correspond with our idea of God. In the hospital illustration, salvation may be put into our hands or poured down our throats like a medicine. In procuring it we are to act like "sensible persons" who know the drug by the label, and who will not buy, even without money and without price, except at the properly recognised establishment. But, what if we think that "the sensible person," whose chief religious motive is to be on the safe side, has corrupted the idea of salvation in every age? He wishes to walk by sight and look after himself, whereas the whole business of salvation is to walk by faith and to be delivered from selfish self-regard. If salvation consists in finding the liberty of the children of God by being enabled to accept God's rule for our own souls, and by being enabled to believe that, in spite of principalities and powers, it will prevail in all things, it cannot be given by any pouring in of grace or any change from without in our natures, or even any kind of moral attainment, whether by effort or sacrament, but must be a turning to God, precisely because we are poor and have no outward trusts. If the one thing needed is utter moral sincerity, an external sacramental institution, restricted to a certain kind of official administration, is too mechanical an instrument to forward our salvation. For that salvation the only adequate sacrament is the whole of life. The Church's observances can only be the symbols and seals and interpretations which show us that all things, if need be the eating of husks, work together for good, when we have found the key to life in loving God.

Yet a movement which has created a new interest in the Christian society and reaffirmed its task, can never be corrected or supplemented by a mere negative denominationalism. The defect is not ecclesiastical but religious, and the immediate need at least is not reunion but a revival of positive ideals. Each society has no doubt something to contribute to the whole, but its ideal of the Christian fellowship, its view of the priesthood of all believers and the relation of the ministry to it, its sense of a duty of contributing some special spiritual good to the kingdom of God, has been too often made subordinate to success as an institution. There is much opportunism, much measurement of spiritual means by material prosperity, much eking out of failures by inconsistent devices. When we believe in institutions in that sense, all justification for weakening the largest by remaining apart from it is taken away.

With this has gone a negative, respectable, middle-class morality which is but imperfectly alive to the dangers of worldliness, pride, and self-indulgence, which is rightly repellent to large masses of the people and which has no real place in its heart for the social outcast and the moral failure.

Moreover, there is a growing tendency to develop the legal spirit of corporations, to accumulate property, to expect to impress by handsome and well-upholstered buildings, and generally to lose the old Puritan idea that the Church must persuade by the gospel and not be impressive by its ceremonial, and that its splendour must be in consecrated lives, not consecrated buildings.

In short, there is a failure to take any deeper grasp of the old Protestant view that the Church must be prepared to lose herself in the common life. The old Erastianism enters in another form. We cannot make the sacrifices which might succour men as our brethren in Jesus Christ, without humility and the utter sense that our whole riches is in God, and without ridding ourselves of caste feeling and seeing its nothingness in comparison with all being children of God. Instead, we have taken to methods of force disguised as public opinion, social censure, or social legislation. In their place these things may be good, but if it means that we have lost faith in the power of ideas, of humble brotherly lives, and of God's kingdom within as the only way of having God's kingdom without, then we have lost the right to believe in any such society as the Church except as a great impressive organised institution. It is simply another phase of the catholicism of the natural man which does not wish to leave anything to God it can help. The result is a temper which is only kept in some measure of Christian meekness and patience by the discipline of division.

To this there is another side. There is earnest search after unity, self-sacrificing service of the kingdom of God, and some movements big with the issues of the future. Such was the creation of the Scottish United Free Church. Like the High Church party, it is determined to maintain the Church as a religious, a Divine society, not to be identified with the civil society, and yet with a national significance on better justification than mere recognition by the State. Moreover, it has willingly paid the price of freedom by abandoning State endowments and State privileges. But only now that it has truly become a national Church has the test of its spirit and of its ideals begun. Will its adversities and the truly Christian willingness to accept self-sacrifice for unity and truth which marked the rank and file, teach the leaders to throw off the legal spirit and rest its ministry on the priesthood of all believers? Will it as a dominant society be able to maintain a humble dependence only on spiritual influences, a moderation in material possessions, a heroic spirit willing to make sacrifices for truth, an independence of judgment which will check the spirit of a large corporation, such as will make it a blessing and not a curse, a bulwark of individual liberty and not of mere corporate force of opinion within the State?

That is a question, it may be, of as much importance for the whole Church of Christ as anything that has arisen since the days of Constantine.

To that end some courageous and consistent thinking on the ideal of the Church is necessary, and that means courageous and consistent thinking on God and on salvation. The present combination of rational and evangelical thinking is everywhere but ill compounded and full of compromises. The immediate task is far more to make clear our ground on such matters, and to know what we believe, than to proceed to ecclesiastical cures for our ills, ecclesiastical cures which usually mean further compounding and compromising.

THE TASK OF THE PRESENT

CHAPTER XII

THE TASK OF THE PRESENT

IF the distinctive principle of the Church consists in its relation to a Divine order of love for which all human history is a discipline and preparation, yet which God alone can introduce, the question of unity must ever be fundamental. But, if unity is tested by its nearness to this Divine order, the organisation of it must be subordinate to the spirit of it, and positive contributions to it be reckoned of more value than the most respectable absence of defects. Sufficient pliability in accepting other people's convictions and a habit of sitting so loosely to ties as not to be galled by other people's fellowship, a spirit of dull mediocrity in ethics, and of uncritical facility of belief, however they cohere in one society, will help men little towards being "perfected into one," which is the only promise of real unity ever given them.

When we are told that our divisions are the scandal and weakness of our Christianity, very frequently no more is meant than that a great organisation would command submission. As such, the Church would exercise authority somewhat after the fashion of the State. But such an authority would in no way forward an order which is to be purely a rule of God, and we can well believe that one of the providential reasons for our present divided state is to bring so external and material a rule to an end. To dismiss our divisions as mere quarrelsomeness and perversity is to be blind to the meaning of history and to lack faith in a guiding hand over human affairs. If progress is no mere process of the ages, no mere cosmic evolution, no mere movement to be gathered up into categories, but a real historical human struggle to understand and apply the ever-present, ever-active revelation of God, and to realise in the end the true rule of God, the interest must be greatest precisely where the ferment is greatest. In that case no age and no country have been more important, at least since the Roman world in the first three centuries, than our own, for here in vigorous interaction are found all the forces produced in the Church from the beginning.

We have recently been told that faith is harmonious spiritual development,* and that too much intellectual activity leads to barren dogmatism, too much feeling to incoherent mysticism, and too much will to ritualistic formalism.† On that view, extremes in religion, all intense insistence on one thing, merely belong to the pathology of the soul, and nothing is left quite certain except the safety of following the maxim, "nothing too much." Apart from the fact that dogmatism exists just to save from real thinking, and mysticism from real feeling, and formalism from real willing, the creative forces in religion are the prophet and the saint and the succourer of his brethren, each waiting on his ministry. The danger is not of touching reality too intensely or even too exclusively at one point, but of refusing to touch reality at all. Men are not kept right in religion by being encyclopædic, but by being sincere. That is the one thing needful to which all else shall

* Professor Inge, "Faith and Its Psychology," p. 223 ff.

† Galloway, "Religious Development," pp. 212–14.

be added, for it will find its fullness of life in God.

It is, therefore, no justification for indifference to any fellow-Christian that we regard him as extreme. The only justification would be to find him insincere, and that conclusion charity should be unwilling to accept, especially if it behold genuine self-sacrifice. Till we are prepared not only to tolerate but to reverence all sincerity, no real tolerance exists, but only at best a contemptuous indifference, which is a far greater breach of Christian charity than the bitterest hatred of what we take to be error. May not one divine purpose in our divisions be just the production in us of a charity which believeth all things on some more Christian ground than the instinct of the herd?

The interest, if a new order is being created, must be where Christianity is most fluid, where opinion and fellowship and organisation are least fixed by rule. And as the finite only approaches the infinite by intense insight into one aspect of truth at a time, we must ever judge by positive contributions and never by limitations and defects. Yet that is true only if all the fruits of the struggle are gathered up into one large fellowship of interest and sympathy, a fellowship into which we may not enter save through the narrow gate of humility, of poverty of spirit, of taking ourselves not to be superior persons but feeble seekers after God.

If only we would steadily regard this as the soul of unity, something might also be done for its body. The radical difference in our views should not be obscured, and we should not pretend that they can be combined. That the ministry is a special priesthood made, by virtue of office, representative of God to rule His people, is one clear view; and that the essence of the Church is a free and equal fellowship of personal faith and its ministry an organ of this equal fellowship, is another. Nothing but confusion of mind can arise from any attempt to combine these two utterly antagonistic positions. We can, however, even here embrace our differences in a mutual charity.

But, if we who hold the latter view had a really deep sense of the unity of the Christian Church, based on the future, not on the past, which we were seeking to realise in all charity, would it be long possible for a large section of our brethren to continue to divide from us on a matter so external as episcopal succession, or for a security so material as the patronage of the State, or to continue to put between us in God's acre and in face of the mystery of death that evil symbol, a broad road?

On the other hand, the recognition that the soul of the Church is union under the direct rule of God, a free, non-legal union of common obedience to His Spirit, and that all organisation is only the body of it, would bring to an end a great many of our divisions, and make us all less ready to divide, by teaching us that we must not expect from the body what is only possible for the soul. Every society should be expected to realise that the Church is different from all other societies in this, that its ideal is its essence. Each society must have an ideal of the Church, and consider in what way it is serving that ideal in its separate state, else it can only exist as a successful corporation without vision of the kingdom of God. When by that test it fails to justify its existence to itself, when it no longer stands alone for the aspect of freedom for which it came into being, it should endeavour, if possible, to bring its isolation to an end.

If the true purpose of the Church is to realise God's rule of freedom through the faith which worketh by love, and amid the imperfections which ever require new disciplines of law, we should have a view of the historical task of the Church which would save us from much division and which would hinder the remaining divisions from cutting so deep into our religious fellowship. Size and social pre-eminence and culture can never be the marks of Christ's Church, and the duty of going out to Christ beyond the camp may at any time arise, and there is no use in healing the hurt of the daughter of Zion lightly by compromises and comprehensive formulæ. But if the Church is engaged in the task of history, of introducing nothing less than God's rule, under which a man may now live in his own soul, and which the world and all the powers thereof cannot hinder him from realising, he will not think it necessary before he can serve the Church to cut himself off from its failures and to endeavour to create a new fellowship corresponding in everything with the ideal, before he can begin. If the Church's task is the task of history, we may not deny responsibility for any branch of the Church, or for the whole struggle, human and passionate and violent as it has been. Unless, under the urgency of very special convictions, we are led to transfer our allegiance, that will mean the duty of serving humbly, patiently, and without striving or crying, the society which first led us into the Christian faith and in whose fellowship we first realised the brotherhood of Christ. But it will also mean that we keep ourselves alive to the whole task of the Christian society and keep open the way to being "perfected into one" in the fulfilment of it, by an interest in all the historic forms of Christianity and a wide charity towards every practical expression of it.

Moreover, if a historic Church is one which realises that it is engaged in a historic task, it may not cut off its members, and especially its ministers, from the intellectual any more than from the moral struggle of our time. To train up its ministry in seminaries, the deliberate purpose of which is to limit their interest to the institution and to give them the intensity in its service of an unquestioned dogmatism protected from the spirit of the age, is simply a rejection of the burden of an historical task at the precise point of history at which God has placed us. For a society to do this and to suppose it conserves its historic position by a doctrine of laying on of hands, is a mockery not only of the modern mind, but of the God who has placed us in the twentieth century, not the twelfth.

That is not walking by faith; and only faith in the reality of God's working can exorcise the legal spirit—which, in spite of all that has been said about mistaken zeal, has been the divisive force—and hazard in belief and action alike the appeal to love which is at once the essence of all union and the whole of the divine order which is embodied in the Church. But with that faith we might look for what is far more important than ecclesiastical unions, a change of ecclesiastical temper. When airs of social superiority ill-becoming those who claim to be the only true successors of the fishermen of Galilee, and resentment and bitterness ill-becoming those who claim to be blessed with the highest ideal of the Church's freedom, pass away, we shall either have outward union, or be so united in heart as to be able to do without it.

If the Church were truly a prophetic society wherein no one needed to say to his brother, Know the Lord, for all knew Him, and no one had any call to be responsible for his brother, because God had written His law on every one's heart, no more would require to be said. But, it will be urged, is it not the historic task of the Church also to train the young, and to give moral guidance to groping and material souls? No church may cast every one not deemed spiritual out of its borders; nay, no church may deny responsibility even for those who deliberately remain outside all churches. Now, can it be questioned that for this ethical, if not religious task, the impressiveness of a large institution saying the same thing and backing one rule of life with its whole impressive authority, is of the utmost value, if not of absolute necessity? The falling away of so many from the organised Christian societies thus raises acutely the whole question of the Church's rule. The cause of the falling away is without doubt the weakening of external authority. An infallible Bible, an unquestioned creed, fear of hell, the official influence of the clergy, were mighty powers to make men submissive members of the Church. Is not the plain lesson, therefore, that the external authority of the Church should again be strengthened? This is the feeling which finds expression in the High-Church movement; and it is by no means confined to that expression, nor is it limited to any one section of the Christian Church.

Yet it is possible to draw another lesson. If, the moment this external authority passes, men cease to care for the Christian fellowship for its own sake, is not the manifest conclusion that, for the propagation of genuine faith, external authority, whether of Bible or Church, must have been of little worth, and that we ought rather to thank God that so slavish a method is no longer possible, and to see that the patient way of calling men to the liberty of the children of God is the quickest way after all? At the same time the effect of large and impressive institutions is very great, and unity and order are necessities of all public and private well-being. It is no part of the Christian spirit to divide as much from others as we choose, so long as we can persuade ourselves that we are right. We ought, therefore, to have grounds for the belief that we have a foundation for a higher unity and a securer order, before we can be indifferent to the power of the Church as one visible, impressive, authoritative organisation. Only if it is the very essence of our faith that we have that foundation in what Professor Gwatkin describes as "the 'inwardness' of Christianity, with its ultra-democratic appeal to the image of God in all men," may we regard this unity as subordinate.

That needs far more than a democratic Church organisation. Christianity is not individualism tempered by the ballot-box. Christ Himself says things little flattering to majorities. A unanimous vote leaves it still possible that God's verdict is on the other side, while the position of an oppressed minority is apparently to continue to be the lot of His real disciples. Christianity is "ultra-democratic" not because it counts heads, but because it appeals "to the image of God in all men." The old Protestant insistence on the priesthood of all believers has lost none of its importance, and the election of the organs of this priesthood by vote may give manifestation to the faith that any brother or sister, however humble or untaught of man, is taught of God. But if the idea is to set up an authoritative, legal ruler, though he be a lay teacher or deacon he is just as much a hierarch as if he were called a bishop and appointed by the State. The idea of election in the Church ought, as at the beginning, to be not any conferring of right upon one man to command another, but the power of a spiritual people to discern spiritual gifts. All authority in the Church must speak only in God's name, and that means neither an appeal to episcopal succession nor to popular election, but solely to truth and the spirit of love. The rulers must be apostles and prophets who believe as the apostles and prophets did, that Christian men are children of God, brethren of each other, spiritual and fitted to judge all things, good soldiers of Jesus Christ who look for victory, not ease, earthen vessels, yet chosen of God and inseparable from His love by the forces of time or eternity. Their appeal shall be unreservedly to the individual, but to the individual in whom the unmerited sense of God's grace has crushed self-assertion, pride, and all insistence upon mere personal rights. In short, their trust shall not be in the power of majorities to back their authority, but in the power of the Christian society to produce what Seeley has described as the only safe foundation for the stable union of liberty and order, "the manhood and moderation which can do without heroes, because it is itself heroic." There we have the eternal basis of fellowship, which, though it is in man, individual man, turns out also to be in God.

But it must never be forgotten that such a basis of order and liberty is heroic and that it can only be appealed to heroically. In other words, it is spiritual and can only be appealed to spiritually. We have to hazard the appeal of simple truth, and not attempt to replace vanishing custom and authoritative beliefs by outward impressiveness. Nothing but the spirit of brotherhood in Jesus Christ and the manifest subordination of wealth and all worldly distinctions to its practical realisation will avail.

The whole question is, whether the Church is a prophetic society because it is historic, or a historic society because it is prophetic. Only on the latter belief can the organisation be thought subordinate to the spirit.

To be founded on the apostles and prophets is not to have a sure traditional link with them which every century must make weaker, but to share in their victory to which every century may contribute. It does not mean that, because they knew God immediately, we may only know Him at second-hand—that, because they recognised God's rule directly, we may only do it indirectly. It means, on the contrary, that through them we also are helped to be apostles and prophets, to hear the Spirit of God's Son in our own hearts and see for our own lives the Divine rule working good through all things. Jesus is the chief corner-stone precisely because He means more for our direct knowledge of God than all others. He gave the creative impulse and abides the supreme inspiration of the Church, because, had He not been crucified from weakness and raised in power, there never could have been a society of those who realise that love alone is victory and are assured that God's rule will come for the world, seeing it has already come for their own hearts and, in spite of all the powers of darkness in this world and the next, for their lives.

This knowledge does not consist in abstract truths about God or in direct impressions from God, but in such insight into His will of love as delivers us from the dominion of all things of outward might. It is neither metaphysical nor mystical, but prophetic, in the sense that it never can be separated from a salvation which is at once victory over self-love and over fear of evil in time and eternity. It is personal but not isolated, being mighty in the society, however few, of those who receive it, and requiring to be kindled at their flame. It is, therefore, both personal and historic, both a sense of our own victory and a sense of an increasing purpose of God.

A metaphysical knowledge of God, providing abstract ideas of the Deity, and a mystical, trusting in influxes of the Divine, can ascribe no religious significance to history. Both alike approach Him as the Absolute. He is supreme organised force. But surely mere omniscience and omnipotence could not fail at all times to convey perfectly an abstract idea or leave its own impress without blur? As that expectation manifestly is not realised in fact, recourse is had to the idea of cosmic process in such a way that history is no longer a real struggle for personal victory or for any spiritual good. The same tendency tempts the less educated to believe that God must somewhere have given an infallibly guaranteed system of truth regarding Himself and a channel of His grace materially secure.

A prophetic knowledge of God, on the other hand, while its first effect is to break down the barrier between us and our fellows, so that we cannot but desire to give them the same knowledge which would equally break down the barrier between them and us, also shows us that, in the strict sense, no one can say to his brother, Know the Lord. There is no real knowledge of God which is not revelation, and there is a sense in which there is no revelation except as to one's own salvation. Precisely because knowledge of God is only second-hand, it is by that very fact not prophetic. It is true indeed that the consecrated individual is the special organ of revelation, and we all depend on him, whether through Scripture or through life, yet it is not to lend us his flame, but to kindle ours.

An abiding realisation of that truth alone can guard the Church in the midst of her temptations "as a teacher of babes." She must kindle in them the spirit of God's children, who, being assured of His rule as their sole environment, are enabled to set above all things the Divine order of love. In that task she is manifestly forwarded only by what lays men's hearts open to the Spirit of God, and in no way by a creed taught authoritatively on pain of perdition, or by the censures of an imposing organisation, or by the secular arm.

Nevertheless, the temptation to use these alien forces, which is so powerful, comes from the fact that nothing can be taught prophetically. Truth has to be taught as doctrine. But, to be of any avail, it must be translated back again into the prophetic knowledge which alone fills it with meaning. In this task, "he that believeth will not make haste," but will know that the responsibility for his brother in the end rests with God and not with him. Yet a form of belief can be used to educe a false sense of responsibility; and then it seems as if something must be won, if only the mere acceptance of doctrines. To that, of course, many kinds of outward authority might contribute.

Did we remember that the task of the Church is always to kindle the soul's own light by bringing God's own fire to it from the altar, we should find guidance regarding her relation (1) to doctrine, (2) to her own organisation, and (3) to the State.

1. If doctrines are merely means for helping men to realise the revelation of God as the unfolding of His will of love, through personal

acceptance of His rule as supreme in power for time and eternity, it is vital that a common conviction speak in them, but there is no particular efficacy in consent to a common form of words. A creed which expresses the living convictions of a church is a spiritual power of the first magnitude; a creed which merely sanctions authorised compromises is not concerned with religion at all, but is a worldly agreement for the legal interest of a corporation.

2. The Church, even in so far as it must be a corporation, should not cherish legal interests. Therein lies the essence of a right relation to her own organisation. The main question is not the kind of ruler, but the kind of rule. It is not whether the organ of the priesthood of all believers is a bishop or a lay deacon. Nor is it determined by the extent of the rule, for the wrong kind of rule may exist in a congregation as well as in a General Assembly or a Convocation. The worst of all kinds of rule of force in the Church would be the dominance of money or rank in the congregation itself, or of wealthier congregations over poorer. Any superiority, indeed, by outward station is hostile to the

fundamental principle of the Christian society, that the first is to be last and the last first. But an appeal on the part even of the official leaders to anything less than the heart of their brethren is also unworthy of a society in which no one is to be called Rabbi.

3. Yet this absence of legal basis does not mean that the Church should not express itself in the world as a society organised on its own basis. She ought rather so to believe in love as the sole organising force of abiding value, that she could not dream of accepting aid from any lower principle, such as organised force in the State. All the material means she may consider necessary to her task she should frankly and fully hold at the disposal of the State, on the understanding with herself that no loss of them can ever touch her true life or even her real organisation. And still more is required, if she is to be an autonomous society in an autonomous State. She may be required to restrict carefully all accumulation of property, and to show that the only possession by which she feels enriched is found in the souls who have been taught to give a secondary place to all material things. The Church must live and work as a corporation, but she must not

magnify herself as a corporation. Rather, like her Master, she must be willing to meet the death of her body, if thereby she may have spiritual power and be a ransom for many. She is to live for the whole society, not by capturing it and ruling it by any means that dazzle and impose, but simply by living humbly her own life in the midst of it.

With that limitation of material power, and with that sense of a mission beneficial to the State, one fitted to help the State itself to appeal less and less to force, carried out by her own method of persuasion and humble service, and restricted to the task of extending this Divine rule in the hearts of men, she may well ask freedom from the State to develop freely her own life. She may even believe that the State also ought to limit itself to the tasks that may be profitably done on its own basis, and that it would mark progress towards a higher organisation of society to afford increasingly scope for every fellowship which seeks other than material good by other means than organised force. Even now, in spite of all their incursions into alien domains, the Free Churches can show, not only that the predictions that tolerance would require a standing army to maintain order have been proved absurd, but that the State has gained much in preferring the loyalty of her children to their subjection.

The Church must, however, recognise ever more clearly that the essence of the civil order is that it is legal, the government of one man by another; while the essence of the religious order is non-legal, the government of a man by his own soul, which is the image of God, and that she may not subject her own higher order to this lower.

At the same time every church ought to be a national church. That is not proved by its presence in every village, being sometimes better proved by its absence. But its eye should be on the nation's needs, not on its own aggrandisement; it should be prepared to serve in the small places as well as the great; it should be found among the poor more readily than among the rich; it should be willing to carry the nation's responsibility in religious things to the ends of the earth.

Were the simple manifestation of God's rule in the Church by the spirit of peace and brotherly love thus made real, there would be less reason to complain of failure and less temptation to fly to lower persuasives.

Does not that appear in the gravest of all outward failures—the failure to retain the great body of the workers? Has it not been in spite of all kinds of organisations and appeals? Every sacrifice has been evident in it, except the only one of any avail—a humble spirit of peace and brotherly love. Condescending ministries and missions of wealthy congregations, convinced that they represent the wise and prudent, scattering money sometimes as impersonally as a charity organisation and sometimes as irresponsibly as tipping, not unnaturally fail to impress the Master's own class with His spirit. Did the Church really manifest things so high that all our little earthly distinctions are levelled by them, and so abundant in goodness that all are poor without them, and all abundantly rich with them, it can hardly be doubted that, as of old, Christ would speak and the common people would hear Him gladly.

The same is true of our greatest inward failure—the discord which still remains between our religion and our morality. Both failures alike arise from failures in our ideas of God and of salvation. To that in the end we always come back. They also are corrupted by the idea of organised force, and divorced from one another, or only attached in arbitrary and legal ways. Instead of beginning with love and realising that love is power, we interpret God primarily as omnipotence and omniscience, and then, in the midst of this resistless flood, some place is sought for the moral personality. Salvation being divorced from the essential nature of God and the realisation of His nature in man, sanctification is no natural fruit of a relation to Him which enables us with meekness to accept His appointments and respond with gladness to His demands, but has to be attached in some arbitrary way. Hopeless logomachies enter about election and man's free-will, in which either God's grace must be restricted or man's personality made void. To save man's moral will, moralistic ideas of merit must be set up; and, the common life having lost its religious meaning as God's dealing with us for our salvation, the exercise of some special discipline must be added, making the relations of religion and morality still more arbitrary.

But these difficulties quite simply fall away from us when we realise that we have to do with a relation of personalities, not forces. Salvation is the succour of our true personality into freedom and the expression of God's essential personality in love. It also interprets for us the Divine government as well as the Divine mind, affording us the key, like nothing else in all the world, to all life's disciplines and duties. Wherefore, we are neither tempted to separate between the Divine succour and our response to it, nor between God's daily appointment for us and the whole Divine will concerning us. Thus we do not so much surmount the difficulties as live in a region where they do not exist. We are able to place the whole stress on God and not on man, yet find our true selves. We can have a faith which empties us of pride, yet gives us genuine self-confidence; which silences self-will and wakens conscience; which shows us how we are enslaved, yet enables us to believe in freedom as God's final purpose with ourselves and the key to all the history of the race.

All that is required of us is to be saints in the old sense of the word—persons who lay themselves open to the Spirit of God, and accept God's rule and suffer it to bring forth in them its own fruits. They are persons, in short, who have faith enough in God to be true to themselves in the lives God has appointed for them, and the duties He requires of them. They have small concern with the might of evil, and are not tempted to worship worldly methods, for God Himself assures to them the kingdoms of this world and the glory of them. God's rule being the environment of their spirits, they need not to strive or cry, but simply need to live in peace as if the kingdom of God were already come for the earth as it has come for themselves.

This temper has not failed. It has not been tried. Perhaps now that so many external supports of Christianity have fallen and we are back at the position before the days when the world took to patronising Christianity, it may have a chance. It will, if we do not say, "The bricks have fallen, but we will build with hewn stones," and say instead, "Not by might, nor by power, but by My Spirit, saith the Lord."

An essential part of this attitude is, without great schemes either intellectual or spiritual, to do our task day by day and trust that God has a greater solution in store than we know. Great confusion has fallen upon us, but let us comfort ourselves with the assurance that progress is not necessarily hindered by failure to understand even ourselves: for if we walk faithfully in such light as is accorded to us, and do cheerfully each day's task as it comes, in all charity, the end and the way will be God's, not ours. Not that church, therefore, which has large schemes of comprehension, will do most to bring near the day of the Lord, but that which is able to say with most power to all its members, in the great words of Luther, "See that thou depart not from the faith that God willeth to do a great work by thee," and to show them that the greatest works are those which abide eternally—faith, hope, and love—and that the greatest of these is love.

INDEX

The Gresham Press,
UNWIN BROTHERS, LIMITED,
WOKING AND LONDON.

Nazarene Theological College
B12845